Vasko Popa

LET'S START OVER AGAIN

Let's Start Over Again

By

VASH YOUNG

Author of
A Fortune to Share

◆

THE BOBBS-MERRILL COMPANY
PUBLISHERS INDIANAPOLIS

Printed in the United States of America

PRESS OF
BRAUNWORTH & CO., INC.
BOOK MANUFACTURERS
BROOKLYN, N. Y.

CONTENTS

LET'S START OVER AGAIN

LET'S START OVER AGAIN

CHAPTER I

LET'S START OVER AGAIN

A WOMAN and her husband stood raking in the ashes of their home. Fire, the day before, had consumed it utterly, and now they were engaged in that heart-breaking search for whatever the flames might have spared. They were shocked, stunned, lost, and in their bewilderment were raking, I suspect, because they did not know what else to do, and not because they had any real hope of salvage. The human mind has a way of turning to trivial action in its efforts to make adjustments to sudden catastrophes.

I never saw a more touching sight than

those two standing there by the side of the road. The flagstone walk led from the roadway to nothing. A tall piece of pipe stood out of the ground, reaching up to where there was no bathroom. Two chimneys, suggestively like gravestones, reared nakedly up into empty space. It made me think of a picture-frame out of which a beautiful canvas had been burned. . . . There is something inexorable, terrible, final about destruction by fire. The man and his wife straightened up, looked this way and that.

"Everything is gone!" said he.

"Yes, everything," added the woman as she sobbed.

A friend came over to them and urged that they get away, for a time, from the scene of their grief.

"But where can we go? What can we do?" asked the woman. "Can't you see that we haven't *anything* left?"

"Oh, yes, you have," insisted the friend.

"What?"

"Well," said he, "you have everything you had yesterday except a house and its equipment. You still have each other, still have your children, your friends, your health and your energy. You still have faith, courage and love. Fire can not destroy these qualities unless you permit it to do so."

"But where are we to live?" asked the man.

"I don't know," answered the friend. "But I do know that you will live somewhere. People always do have somewhere to live. A little thing like a fire doesn't mean that they must spend the remainder of their days out in the woods. If it did the woods would be full of homeless folk, for there have been lots of fires. I tell you what, come stay with us. My wife and I would be delighted to have you, as would scores of other friends."

"But think of being dependent!" said the woman.

"You'll not be," contended the friend. "I repeat, you have not lost anything by this fire except a house and its equipment. That loss is great or small according to the way you think of it. It is a defeat or it is a challenge. What are you going to do: give up and grieve, or fight and win a fine victory? You had energy and ability enough to build that house. Well, you still have the same amount of energy and ability. Why, this is a real chance to show the stuff you are made of! You can win the lasting admiration of your friends, or take a sort of gloomy pleasure in the sympathy extended to you. Temporary sympathy, for it is not nearly so lasting as admiration. If you had lost love, faith or courage I'd say you were in a bad fix. But you have lost nothing but *things*, and things can be replaced."

Obviously, the friend was correct. If that couple had stopped then, as they did later, to figure out their losses and their remaining possessions they would have found themselves thoroughly solvent in all the assets that really matter. Not one permanent thing had they lost. Not one irreplaceable necessity. Not a single eternal reality. Destructible material things are but the products of imperishable spiritual qualities. Every affirmative quality which has enabled life to continue on this earth, and to progress steadily from lower to higher planes of existence, that couple still possessed. Only by being wilfully negative can such qualities be lost. A fire, of course, is very disconcerting, but it need not be disastrous. It is one of those breaks in the continuity of life which can be turned to advantage, for it may be accepted as a test of character, as a challenge to victory over odds. It burns a lot of junk in our attics and cellars which is useless, but which we haven't had the courage to throw away. It may also, if we will, burn a lot of junk in our minds. It offers a great chance to start over again, materially and mentally. And out of new starts come life's great romances.

I saw this couple again the next day, and at the scene of the fire. What a change there was! They had thought it over and had concluded that, after all, they were luckier than most people in that they had more of the genuine assets, the real necessities of life, than go to the common run of humanity. Now their children were with them, and they were discussing the best location for the new house. The old one had not been very convenient. The woman always had wished it back from the road a greater distance, and in a lovely grove of trees which stood there. Also she had wished for another arrangement of her kitchen and dining-room, and for stairs that were less steep. But these desires she had had to put away. Now she found that out of a crisis had come the opportunity to get the kind of home her heart longed for. So, in their plans for the future, they forgot the grief of the past. Overnight their lives had turned around from negative to positive, from fright of the future to high hopes. It is almost always like that when a crisis is met bravely, for nearly every crisis gives us the choice of victory or defeat, of showing admirable or weak attributes of character, of sitting down in sorrow or driving ahead in happy faith.

This couple did, of course, acquire another house in which they now are established in more comfort than they had known in the old place. They are merry and delight endlessly in the many neighbors who stop by to congratulate them on what they have accomplished. By their example they have set an entire community to talking about the things that people can do when faced with what, superficially, might look like ruin.

I have thought of them hundreds of times this past year. As they drooped there amid material losses they illustrated perfectly, visibly and dramatically the situation in which millions of people now find themselves; for fire, figuratively speaking, has visited nearly every home in this country, and in the world. Every one is challenged by material losses. Every one faces the necessity to start over again. Right now is the time to do it!

Right now is the time for every gloomy person, every worried person, every scared person to sit down and list in one column his losses, in another his assets. The losses will include money, probably some luxuries and maybe a dash of pride. The permanent assets will include love, strength, faith, family, friends and so on through a list too long to be enumerated. Every man, woman and child in these United States is solvent, spiritually, or can be. Every normal person in this great land is perfectly capable of starting all over again and building upon the wreckage of the past a finer life than the old one.

Life never has been dependent on booms, inflated values, extravagance, speed and the like. It is, always has been and will be for ever dependent on values within us; upon affirmative qualities of mind and of heart. Battles are won by courage, by attacking again and again; never by fear, worry, grief or that state of collapse which I may best describe as giving up. It is an old, old statement, and more true than old, that life is what you, the inner you, choose to make it.

When this miserable depression got well under way and every one became shrouded in gloom, I realized that it was necessary for me to think and to act more clearly than ever before. I saw that the business situation was serious from a material view-point. I came face to face again, as I had done earlier in my career, with the glorious fact that I could fashion my own life. I realized that the huge economic problems of the times were beyond my control. What could I, the individual, do about tariffs? About international debts? What could I, Vash Young, do about over-production, under-consumption, inflated prices, deflated prices, the gold standard? Mighty little! But there was something I could do. While I could not control these immense forces at work in the world, *I could control their effect on my inner self*. I could set up my own golden standard of character and of view-point, and stick by that, come what may.

"No matter what happens," I said, "I'll not let the depression get *inside* me. It may rage all around me. I can't help that. But I am the keeper of my own inner self, and I'll shut and lock the doors to my mind every time I apprehend the approach of a gloomy thought. I'll not judge others because of their conduct, but I'll be a hard-boiled judge of my own."

I have a way, when facing a problem, of talking to myself. It helps to fix my own conclusions in my mind. It helps to drive out and away thoughts which I do not wish to remain with me. It helps to keep my mind open and hospitable to good thoughts, those that are unselfish, active, affirmative, and to render it forbidden ground to all sour direful imaginings. Also I have that way I have mentioned of listing my assets now and then. A sort of personal bookkeeping for the guidance of my own conduct. I write down all the things I have that are worth having, and in another place I put down those things that are worthless; then I declare war on the worthless items. Among the assets I listed when this depression came along was my memory of a newspaper paragraph which I had seen somewhere many years ago, and in the course of a financial crisis. Here it is:

"This truth within your mind rehearse—
to talk hard times will make times worse."

I am not one of those foolish men who refuse to face the facts. I know that almost every person in the United States has less of the non-essential material things than he had three years ago. I also know that material possessions are convenient, comforting, in a way, and very dear—too dear—to the hearts of many persons. I know that I must work harder than ever before, think more of the view-point of the other fellow, meet with what, to some, would be failure after failure. But I differ from those who list the failure to get an order as a failure. To me, the only possible source of failure is within me. It does not matter vastly what happens to the outer man, so long as the inner man maintains himself on the highest attainable plane. Long ago I stopped worrying about the outer man. It seems obvious to me that worry is one of the silliest occupations of mankind. If this belief lands me, eventually, in the poorhouse I'll handle that situation after I get there, but I'm bound and determined not to live in a lot of "mental poorhouses" meanwhile. Incidentally, my philosophy, so far, has not taken me anywhere near a poorhouse. I have escaped losses, which convinces me that my view-point of life is wise materially as well as spiritually. I have no more ability than the average man. I have less education than the average, for I did not finish the sixth grade. In size, physical strength and appearance I'm about average. I can not, therefore, attribute my escape from the depression as due to any of these things. It must be that my attitude, my philosophy, my faith, my mastery of my own emotions has made me able to keep on doing as much business in depressed as in boom times.

Every week I talk with scores of persons who are in trouble. Most of them, nine out of ten, are worried about money. Many have lost their jobs. Others have had cuts in pay. But every one who comes to me still has life, most of them have health, and all of them either have, or could regain, faith and courage. Some of the stories related to me are heartrending: A hard-working woman, now along in years, had saved all of her days against the time when she could earn no more. Her savings are gone now, through no fault of her own. A young man who got married on the promise of a raise in pay, and then was fired. A girl whose mother looks to her for support now finds herself with no income. There is an endless list of these callers, many from distant states, and every one of them deserving of sympathy, every one needing to make a new start, but momentarily so confused they do not know in what direction to set out. I am powerless to give them jobs or money. My only hope is to give them a view-point which may help them to jobs and money, and which certainly will lighten their loads of worry.

For a great many years Saturday, as readers of *A Fortune to Share* may remember, has been "Trouble Day" in my office in New York. This means I give that day to callers who come hoping I may assist them. Hundreds and hundreds have come, and every last one confesses that he has made matters worse by worry. Not yet have I found a person who claims any good thing for worry. It only increases one's misery. Some say they can not help worrying. I know they can. I *know* that the processes of the mind are subject to control. Not complete control in every case, perhaps, but partial control, at the least. I have gained dominion over my emotions, and what is possible for me certainly is possible for others. Years ago I determined that never again would I make bad matters worse by indulging in self-pity, lamentation, worry or any other bad habit that might destroy me. Worry does nothing except weaken initiative, dull the sparkle in the eye, drive out hope and sap courage. Where there is too much worry, the cause is lost.

Chaotic conditions have got to be met in

one way or another, and they might as well be met as a challenge to stability and character. That's how I try, always, to meet them. I can see no sensible reason why any man should invite disaster by allowing his own mental processes to work against him. So far as you are concerned a condition is what you think it is. Take this depression. Is it unbearable? Does it justify dense gloom? Does it give any person the right to be a blight on the happiness of those around him? Does it offer any real excuse for accepting defeat? Some one has said, and rightly, that the depression means merely that we must do without a few things which our grandparents never dreamed of having.

Even when I was a child—and I'm not an old man, nor do I ever intend to be!—out in Salt Lake City we had nothing more than the bare necessities of life, yet we thought little of it. A boy who had money enough to see a circus once a year was lucky. I went weeks and even months without a penny in my pockets, and did not know that the absence of money was a hardship. Why, matches, in those days, were considered a luxury. We knew nothing of course of these tricky lighters done in all sorts of ornate metals and often in precious metals. We made our own baseballs, our own bats, played without gloves and had a swell time of it! Very few gadgets were then thought essential. I know, therefore, out of my own experiences that life can be lived without all the things now thought necessary.

But life can not be lived without courage, nor could it ever be. Such unhappiness as I knew when a child, and later after I grew up, was never due to lack of money, though I had none. It all came from the wrong view-point, from worry, dissipation of energy, fear of the future, regret for the past.

I became thoroughly happy long before I had any money at all, and even when I had no job and did not know where the rent for next month, nor the food for next month, nor the clothes for myself and my wife, were coming from. Happiness came to me almost the instant I turned around, started over again with a vow to live courageously, optimistically, unselfishly; when I stopped thinking of my own petty affairs and threw myself whole-heartedly into the grand adventure of living an affirmative life. Material comforts came later and as a result, I believe, of the mental conquest already achieved.

One Saturday morning an artist came in to talk with me. He had been locked out of his studio because he could not pay his rent. He had no commissions on hand. He was sick at heart, lost in the fog generated in his own gloomy mentality. He told me his story. Yes, obviously he was an artist, for none other could have used such terrible colors in painting personal problems.

"Well," I said when he had finished, "I guess your situation is hopeless. Conditions have finally become too much for God Himself."

"What's that?" exclaimed the artist in a startled tone.

"Yes," I went on, "conditions are so bad that God is pacing up and down in Heaven wondering what to do about the terrible mess things have got into."

"That's blasphemy!" shouted my caller. "Never in my life have I heard such fool talk!"

"Maybe it is blasphemy," I answered, "but it is not so blasphemous as your present attitude. That picture of God I have given to you is taken from your own character as you show it to me. The Bible says you are made in His image. If that's right, if you are His image, He certainly is pacing up and down wondering what to do about His rent and about everything else."

"For heaven's sake," he begged, "don't let's drag the Almighty into such talk!"

"And for heaven's sake," I answered reverently, "don't let us, who are made in His image and likeness, go about our affairs, expressing the very opposite of what He is. One day of being like God in the things we think and do is more important than a year of prayer for undeserved blessings. We know that He is not sick, depressed, worried, fretful and weak. If He were, this world would have failed long ago. Can you imagine the Creator in your present image?"

"Hardly!"

"Can you imagine yourself being more like Him than you now are?"

"Of course."

"Well, then, it seems to me you have hit

on the solution for your internal problems, even if not on the solution of your rent problem. You certainly do not have to go around disgracing the God in whom you profess to believe by manifesting all of the attributes which would, if universally practised, result in the destruction of the race of man."

In the end we agreed that what he needed, first of all, was to change his mental attitude toward his situation. He needed to apply some of the common-sense rules of salesmanship to his profession. It happens that I am a salesman, and so I was able to impress on him the importance of calling on a prospect in the right frame of mind.

"Have you any prospects now?" I asked.

"Yes, an old lady said she might have her portrait painted."

"Have you called on her recently?"

"No."

"Why not?"

"I was afraid she might refuse."

"She certainly would have refused if you had approached her in that state of fear."

He left my office with his chin up, called on the lady, made such a fine impression on her that she paid him, that very afternoon, six hundred and fifty dollars in advance on the portrait he was to make. He opened up his studio, and started working all over again. All that happened in his case was the replacement of worry with hope, of fear with courage. By *thinking* right he produced what we call "the breaks."

Can every one do this in every case? I do not know. But I do know that right thinking produces good results often enough to make it plain nonsensical not to try it. Also, I know that fearful thinking, gloom-spreading, worry and all their black-draped kindred emotions never have produced anything worth-while in my life or in my line.

"Give yourself a chance!" That's what I urge on people who come to me in distress. "You can't possibly do anything in your present state of mind. You have started running in a destructive circle. You find yourself doing nothing, therefore you worry yourself into uselessness, and because of that you can not do anything. The circle must be broken. The place to break it is in your own thinking. Give yourself a chance!"

A very disconsolate man came in one day to see me.

"What's wrong?" I asked, for I could see from the expression on his face that he thought something had become unhooked.

"Everything is wrong," he answered.

"Everything?"

"Yes, everything under the sun."

I took from my desk a little piece of paper upon which one paragraph was typed. It had been written by Chase S. Osborn, former governor of Michigan and now one of America's most colorful and hopeful philosophers. He had written it in a letter to a friend of his.

"You ask when things are going to be better," read the paragraph. "I might retort by asking *what* things? There is absolutely nothing wrong with the earth. The sun performs its functions. The earth is still in its orbit and on its axis. The clouds that are the nursemaids of the sky move hither and thither as usual and drench the thirsty footstool. The soil has all the elements of nourishments that sustain human life and everything else that it ever had. There is nothing wrong with the earth and with heaven, but somewhere between there has been a good deal of a mess. What then *is* wrong? It must be man!"

I handed this paragraph to my caller and he read it slowly.

"What do you think of it?" I asked him.

"Good reading," he answered, "but what has it got to do with my case?"

"It tells you where the trouble is," I said.

"Yes, but what about my own situation? I'm not much interested in things in general."

"Then we'll have to make it specific," I said. "The trouble is with man. Your own trouble is with one man. That one man is yourself."

"What do you mean by that?"

"I mean that you have pressed the wrong buttons, turned on the wrong taps. Everything you have done since you came into this office shows you have surrendered to discouragement and to bad temper. My secretary told me that even before you got in here you were scolding about the long wait, worrying about the rain outside, wondering when people would have sense enough to put rubber tires, or something, on street-cars so they would not make so much noise. Now, how can you expect to get anywhere in that state of mind? I'm wondering when some people will have sense enough to know they can't solve their problems by intensifying them through worry, anger and fear."

"I didn't come here to get bawled out," he said hotly. "I came because a friend told me you would help me, and I need help."

"I'll say you need it!"

"Well, then, how about giving me a little help?"

"All right. Here it is: Start all over again in your hunt for a job, but before going outside of this room, change your disposition and your view-point. I can't give you a job, my friend, but I can tell you something that is worth a thousand jobs. You need to work on yourself before you start working for anybody else."

"I get you," he admitted, "but things have been so bad with me that I've soured."

"Which is to say you have made bad matters worse."

"Exactly!"

And that's what millions of others have done! Why do people act stupidly when they know they are being stupid? As I've said, not one person I have seen had any good word for worry, surrender, bad temper, but nearly every one is the victim of one or more of these handicaps. The human race could not survive on such qualities. It has survived, and progressed, because of other and stronger traits, but the progress has been hindered by these weaknesses. To me it seems just plain unintelligent to permit, to invite, personal disaster when there is no compulsion on us or in us to extend the invitation.

I like to think of a little old couple in the South who have reversed the rule of pessimism. I called on them one day because I had heard of their plight, and thought perhaps I could offer a word of cheer. But I discovered that I had nothing for that couple. It was I, not the old lady and the old man, who became richer because of my chance visit. I went into their shack, I'm ashamed to say, feeling a little like a reformer; I came out humbly reformed in spirit, for here is what I saw, and what I learned:

The man of this shack is confined to a wheel-chair, and his wife is none too able to do all that she must do. At one time they had been well off in money, but now they were destitute.

"They have nothing at all," some one had told me, but I soon discovered that they had the greatest wealth of spirit I had met with in many months. I had expected to find unhappiness; instead I found a sort of quiet radiance. I had expected old people either petulant or martyr-like; instead I found them merry.

Last Christmas the story I am telling came to its beautiful climax.

"I think we should have a Christmas tree," the old lady suggested.

"We haven't a thing in this wide world to put on it," said her husband. "Still, if you want a tree I guess we can have one. Some of the schoolboys will cut it for us and put it up."

The boys of the vicinity were glad to do this, as the shack of these old folks was a favorite gathering place for children. The tree was set up, the boys who did the work told about it, and things began to happen in a hurry. A neighbor came in and asked for the privilege of decorating the tree. Another asked that she be permitted to supply Christmas dinner. The spirit of hope, of courage, of refusal to surrender to hard conditions spread about, and when Christmas Day arrived the little shack in the woods became the center of festivities.

"Say, if those little old folks can be as brave as that," said one visitor, "I certainly am not going to cringe any more as I've been doing. They make me ashamed. Why, I have a thousand times as much as they, and I've been spreading nothing but gloom!"

A wealthy woman who was there confessed that, in her own home, they had decided to have no Christmas at all because they could not afford it. Could not afford to be happy! And with a hundred thousand times as much money as this feeble old couple had. Not only that, but with youth, health and opportunity to make the future better than the past.

"Please, please!" said this woman. "Don't say anything to me. I feel badly enough as it is!"

What brought about that miracle there in the woods? Well, in the first place it was not a miracle. It was the natural expression of the heart at its best. It was but the evidence of faith, hope and courage, and steadfast refusal to become sour. Just a simple case of making the best of what seemed a hopeless situation.

Every community in the United States has such heroes. There is not a village anywhere that has not in it a magnificent story of courage, a story that should shame all the neighbors out of their agonizing worry over material losses. Shame them, and also illustrate to them how unintelligent it is to make matters worse than they need be. If you already are up to your ears in trouble, why walk out into deeper waters of worry and fear? The choice is a deliberate one.

Often I go about making speeches. It is not my wish nor my job to do so, but many people, it seems, want to hear why I got tired of being a fool, how I started over again, and what is the fortune, the mental fortune, I have to share. On these trips I meet with many brave souls and hear many brave stories. There is the instance of an old man who lived alone for twenty years. He had nothing, so people said, but what they meant was that he had no money except a few dollars a month on which he subsisted. Actually he had enough merriment, enough bravery and enough comforting philosophy to be a blessing, instead of a care. Everybody liked him. No one ever had seen him fretful. One evening a friend went into his rooms and found him preparing supper. At the kitchen table three places were set.

"Having company to-night?" asked the friend.

"I always have company," answered the old man.

"Why, I thought you lived alone!"

"Oh, no, I'm never alone. My wife died and my boy died many years ago, but always I set those places for them at the evening meal. Some folks think I'm out of my head to do it, but I don't think so. I like to do something visible to show that they are with me yet in my consciousness. That keeps me from being lonely."

Another miracle? Not at all. Merely another instance of the power of love to sweeten life. Another instance of a brave soul. That old man might have been, and with some excuse, the most miserable person on the top side of the earth. Instead, he chose to be happy, and he was. He preferred a romantic to a pathetic life, victory to defeat. Success to failure. The choice was his to make.

Some years ago a friend of mine permitted his oldest son, a splendid boy, to go on an outing with some other boys and a man. Through an accident the son of this friend was killed. The tragedy threw the whole town into mourning, and there were many who blamed the man in charge of the group. The bereaved father and mother heard this opinion expressed, and the father came out on to his front porch where neighbors had gathered, for it was the night of the boy's death.

"Is Mr. So-and-So here?" he asked.

"Yes," some one answered. "He's out there under the trees."

"Ask him to come in."

His head hanging, the man who had taken those boys to walk came into the light.

"My wife and I," began the grief-stricken father, "wish you to know that we do not think this your fault. I am sure you were as careful of my son as I would have been. We hope you will not let the accident worry you too much."

The father turned then and went back into the house, while a score of men standing there on the porch gasped in their admiration of this generous conduct. Even in their grief, these parents had thought of others, had demonstrated the magnificence of the human heart at its best.

The years passed. The story of this supreme self-control was told and told again. The man and his wife grew mightily in the estimation of their neighbors. They had set an example of right thinking, an example which helped them to meet their own tragedy, and which has helped scores of others to face the critical moments of life with fortitude. Courage is like that. It blesses those who have it, and those who behold it. The influence of it lasts for ever.

I have a theory about this depression, a plan for its relief. Thousands of other plans have been suggested, most of them dealing with economic matters. Some of them, no doubt, are quite sound. But my plan has very little to do with abstract or abstruse matters. You will not find it in books on economics, nor does it call for any action by law-making bodies. It has nothing to do with unconsumed surpluses, with the gold standard, with taxation or with tariffs. It does not call for much study, nor for much education of the formal sort.

Here it is:

Set your own mind in order. Forget greed, discard fear. Do every day the very best you can do in every situation. Be energetic, be unselfish, be happy.

If one hundred and twenty million of us followed that course, would the depression last long? It simply could not, for how can there be depression if every one refuses to be depressed? Let's get down to fundamentals. What are the qualities that have enabled us to advance to where we are? Gloom? Agony? Terror? Pessimism? Hoarding? Doubting the future? Questioning the ability of mankind? Denouncing others? Accepting defeat as inevitable? Not a bit of it! The progress made in this world is based, always, on courage, love, imagination, unselfishness, honesty, religion. These qualities in individuals make the world go ahead. There is no sense in waiting for somebody else to do something. Do something yourself about yourself. When millions of individuals emerge from sticky gloom, the country will emerge with them, will it not? Of course it will, for individuals make up the country. Therefore I have said to myself:

"Come on, it is time for you to start over again!"

What would happen, I wonder, if every

man said the same thing to himself, and meant it? The answer seems to me to be very clear. An untold lot of things would happen, and they'd be good things, too.

Chapter II

NEW ACTORS ON AN OLD OLD STAGE

If you have been to Ringling's circus within the past few years you must recall those Ugandi savages, black people from Africa who, for some crazy reason, stretch their lower lips until they are as big as pancakes. These huge lips stick almost straight out in front of the mouth. This distinguishes them from the lower lips of a great many business men which hang down until there is danger of their owners stepping on them. I have seen a few bankers with expressions so sad that any depositor would have been justified, after taking one look, in withdrawing his money and running with it. I heard an executive say to one of his assistants, who had come in with a new plan to arouse customers, that he might try it or not as he chose.

"It will not do any good," said the executive, "but neither will it cost anything. If it will make you happier, try it. As for me, I think we are sunk, and that the country is sunk!"

An advertising agent came to me one day and asked if I knew where he might find a good client.

"I'm about to give up hope," said he. "Unless I find a new client soon I'll begin asking about the best bread-line etiquette."

"If you feel that way about it," I said, "I'll not only hunt a client for you, but I'll guarantee to find one."

"Lead me on!"

"Tell me, first, what is your procedure when you land a new client?"

"Why, I analyze his business, study the nature of his existing and potential customers, find out his strong points, his weak ones, study his successful competitors—you know, all that kind of thing. Then I show him how to put up a real fight for business."

"Fine!" said I. "And here's the name and address of the best client you ever had."

I handed him a slip of paper.

"Say, what's the big idea? You have given me my own name and address."

"Yes," I said, "and I did it because that is the most valuable client you can have at this particular time. Go ahead and analyze your own affairs, study the nature of your own customers and potential customers, find out your strong points, your weak ones, study your successful competitors—you know, all that kind of thing. Then put up a real fight for business! This talk about giving up is the bunk. It's sinful—silly."

Scared to death! Either that, or smothering in doleful thoughts. That's what has been the trouble. And scared of what? Grieving about what? The loss of money and some of the things money will buy. Men are not afraid to die when there is a great emergency calling for the supreme sacrifice. I once knew a man who had run away from business obligations he could not, at the moment, cope with. He was in no disgrace. Everybody was on his side, but he could not stand the thought of going broke, so he sought sanctuary in some rather remote mountains. One day as he stood on the shore of a lake he saw a canoe upset far out from shore, and the man who had been in the canoe seemed to be sinking. In an instant this scared business man had taken off his clothes and dived into the cold water. Strongly he swam out toward a stranger in trouble, risking his life eagerly, for the water was bad that day, both cold and rough. The rescue was made, and the rescuer seemed to think nothing of it. Yet he was afraid of losing money! The mind is capable of some extraordinary paradoxes.

We are facing to-day nothing more than an economic emergency, a bad one, I'll admit, but it can not destroy us. Death rates actually have decreased since the coming of "hard times." Divorce rates also have decreased. There has been a fine spirit of mutual sacrifice and mutual assistance which has brought together many an estranged couple these past few years. Thousands of men have become acquainted with their own children. It looks to me, therefore, as if there is some good in all this mess we are in. Still, millions go around with sagging lips, sagging hopes, sagging courage.

The human race is not going to fail all of a sudden. It has stood up under worse conditions than these, and in the days when there was less knowledge. Civilization, thousands of years in the making, can not be unmade in a decade. Our national spirit, which means the aggregate of our individual spirits, is not going to turn craven overnight and permit disaster. Certainly I do not intend to invite any disaster to befall me. I don't like it, and I'm going to fight it off. Nobody likes it, but it does seem, at times, as if some were not trying to fight it off.

"How are you feeling?" I asked a manufacturer.

"Terrible," he answered. "Simply terrible."

"What's wrong, your wife sick?"

"No."

"Your children sick?"

"No."

"Been sentenced to jail?"

"Oh, stop it!" he said. "You know what's

wrong as well as I do. There never has been any such situation as this before."

"Take a vacation," I suggested, "and read your history. It might do you some good. It can't very well do you any harm."

"Maybe you are right," he admitted. "Anyway, I'd like to read something that is not written in red ink."

The story of mankind, as every one knows, is not written in red ink. There have been hundreds of wars, thousands of blunders, countless setbacks. And there have been many business depressions. But gains have outweighed losses, always, in the long run. Otherwise there would have been retrogression, instead of progress. Take these depressions, or panics, as we call them, and often they are depressions because they are panics. Panics in the minds of men. They come now and then, but what is more to the point, they go. Yes, every last miserable depression, so far, has vanished into oblivion. This one also will move out and away. The course of the thing is about run now, but it will linger on until we, the individuals, do something about our inner lives, our viewpoints. When we decide it is over, the turn will have come. Within the past few years the prediction has been made thousands of times that better conditions were just around the corner, and a few persons peeped fearfully around to see if it were true. That's no way to win a victory over depression. Courage, rather than a cautious glance, is needed. I must act, you must act. We can not afford to wait for somebody else to solve our problems for us. I see the present as a distinct challenge to every one. It is to the advantage of each one to win the victory as soon as possible. Therefore the intelligent thing to do is to fight. Campaigns are not won on fear or worry or too much caution.

Thomas Macaulay, writing in 1830, spoke of the state of mind then existing.

"The present moment is one of great distress," said he. "But how small will that distress appear when we think over the history of the last forty years; a war, compared with which all other wars sink into insignificance; taxation such as the most heavily taxed people of former times could not have conceived; a debt larger than all the public debts that ever existed in the world added together. . . .

"Yet is the country poorer than in 1790? We believe firmly that, in spite of all the misgovernment of her rulers, she has been almost constantly becoming richer and richer. Now and then there has been a stoppage, now and then a short retrogression; but as to the general tendency there can be no doubt. A single breaker may recede; but the tide is evidently coming in."

Sounds like to-day, doesn't it? Read some more from the same man and the same essay:

"To almost all men the state of things under which they have been used to live seems to be the necessary state of things. . . . We cannot absolutely prove that those are in error who tell us that society has reached a turning point, that we have seen our best days. But so said all who came before us, and with just as much apparent reason. On what principle is it that, when we see nothing but improvement behind us, we are to expect nothing but deterioration before us?"

There must have been a business depression on in those days, and Macaulay was trying to show people that all they needed do was to take a new grip on life, look ahead and start ahead. The only way we can estimate the future is by studying the past; the past has been mainly good. The sensible course, therefore, is to decide that the future will be mainly good and live hopefully to-day. I can't do anything about yesterday, nor can I project myself into to-morrow. But to-day is with me now, and my job is to make the best of it. If every to-day is made a success, there is no cause to grieve over the past or doubt as to the future.

Back in 1857 these United States had a real depression, and voices were raised in doleful tones. This, surely, was the end of a promising experiment—America. Liberty had been won. A vast and rich domain waited to be used. But here is how a writer of those times looked at events:

"It is a gloomy moment in history. Not for many years—not in the lifetime of many men who read this paper (*Harper's Weekly*)—has there been so much grave and deep apprehension; never has the future seemed so incalculable as at this time. In our own country there is universal commercial prostration and panic and thousands of our poorest fellow citizens are turned out against the approaching winter without employment, and without the prospect of it.

"In France the political cauldron seethes and bubbles with uncertainty; Russia hangs, as usual, like a cloud, dark and silent upon the horizon of Europe; while all the energies, resources and influence of the British Empire are sorely tried, and are yet to be tried more sorely, in coping with the vast and deadly Indian insurrection and with its disturbed relations in China.

"It is a solemn moment, and no man can feel an indifference (which, happily no man pretends to feel) in the issue of events.

"Of our own troubles no one can see the end. They are, fortunately, as yet mainly commercial; and if we are only to lose money, and by painful poverty to be taught wisdom—the wisdom of honor, of faith, of sympathy and of charity—no man need seriously despair. And yet the very haste to be rich, which is the occasion of this widespread calamity, has also tended to destroy the moral forces with which we are to resist and subdue the calamity.

"Good friends—Let our conduct prove that the call comes to men who have large hearts, however narrowed their homes may be; who have open hands, however empty their purses. In times of peril we have nothing but manhood, strong in its faith in God, to rely upon; and whoever shows himself truly a God-fearing man now, by helping however he can, will be blessed and loved as a great light in darkness."

That, also, sounds like to-day, doesn't it? These commercial deflations seem to be fairly well standardized. The United States has lived through at least eight of them. Often they run something like this: Prices become too high, then tumble. For a time the public, excited over easy gains, will not admit the reality of the fall. False optimism breaks out, to be followed by pessimism greater than warranted. The pendulum that has swung too far in one direction, swings back too far in the other. There is panic, there are predictions that the whole social structure will collapse. There is paralyzing inactivity, together with confusing yells that somebody else do something. Then the mind turns again to common sense. Courage begins to rise, activity begins anew, and the depression is on its way to the showers, knocked out of the box.

The panic which followed the War of Secession was singularly like our own pet panic of to-day, both in cause and in effect. War had speeded production beyond normal needs, but the waste and excitement of war had taken care of the surpluses. Peace came, and with it extravagance, political incompetence, dishonesty in many high spots and a general letting down of moral and mental tension. Then the financial crash.

Henry Ward Beecher, that robust preacher of those days, delivered a famous lecture dealing with the panic of 1873. He called his lecture *Hard Times*.

"What is the matter?" he demanded. "What has happened? Why, from the very height of prosperity, without any visible warning, without even a cloud of the size of a man's hand on the horizon, yet a cloud appeared, as it were from the center first, spreading all over the sky. And very many reasons have been given. Some men have found either in the presence of the tariff, or in the fact that the tariff was not screwed up high enough; that it was too high, too low, or something—that there was a cause.

Other men have found that it was overproduction; that we created beyond the power of consumption, food, raiment and all the material of life. Other men have thought that the trouble came from luxury; that men had grown profuse in expenditure. . . . Others think that the whole thing lies in the fugitive nature of confidence. . . ."

There again, we have words which sound like those being spoken now. The great preacher then continued:

"I think that men have learned that industry must be applied to produce wealth, not speculation. Young men are coming up with better ideas, and willing to work. . . . Oh, how many men live a life without ever finding out what the golden secret of happiness is! That a man's life is in his own family, under his own roof, and in the commerce of sweet, pure affections."

The good doctor might have added a

phrase to that last sentence. He might have said that a man's life is in his own family, under his own roof, within his own consciousness and in the commerce of sweet, pure affections.

In his heart every person knows that he has more cause for contentment than for gloominess, but into our thinking counterfeit values have intruded. We can not have sunk so low in intelligence that courage and hope are dependent upon money in the bank. It is a convenient, a comforting, a necessary thing to have, but its possession depends on mental and spiritual qualities, not they on it.

This always has been true. It is true today. There is not a thing new about these problems which worry so many people. They are standardized, if that word may be used to describe them. Even depressions, as we have seen, are standardized. Greed for easy gains, fear, doubt—they have come down through the ages hampering happiness, as they hamper it now. Unselfishness, courage, faith—they, too, have come down through the ages, conquering their opposites, as they will conquer them now if we give them the chance. New actors, that is all we are, on an old, old stage. We may dress in a manner not like that of ages past, we may speak differently from our ancestors, live in houses that are different. But fundamentally life does not change. We still must win food and shelter, and to win them we still must work and hope. Human needs always have existed, and always will. They are the same basic needs, always. To fill them the same basic efforts, in the mind and with the body, are required now that were required long ago. There is nothing, speaking of fundamentals, that is new under the sun, nor is any new thing needed. All that is needed is to use the faculties we possess in the way intelligence and experience tells us to use them.

Newspaper head-lines always interest me. As I have gone about over the country this past year I have made a point of studying them. They reveal the public attitude, I presume, and reflect the public interests. I have noticed that my fellow newspaper readers often seem disappointed if there is no news bad enough to justify scare heads. On a train recently I was in the dressing-room with several other men. The train stopped and a news boy came through. A passenger who had finished with his shaving bought a paper and started to read it.

"Any news?" some one asked.

"No," he answered. "Not anything fit to read."

"What! No murders, scandals, business failures or anything like that?"

"No, the world seems to have taken the day off yesterday," and he tossed the paper on to the seat beside him. When he left the room I picked it up to see what it was that did not interest him. Here are a few of the items which, according to his taste, were not fit to read: An important discovery in science, the passage by Congress of some remedial legislation, a rescue at sea, a statement by somebody that American women are the most beautiful in the world, and an aviation speed record. There were other items, too, many of them about normal life. But it so happened that there was no item sufficiently sensational, sufficiently discouraging, or sufficiently scandalous to demand a huge type display. Now, what has happened to that man's appetite? The same thing that has happened to millions of other appetites—he has had his taste spoiled for the normal. Which means that he has, temporarily, become uninterested in wholesome news. This love of the sensational was fed to the fullest back in the days of the World War. Every one then became accustomed to scare heads, and after the war had ended, the public still wanted excitement. There came along the revolution in manners and morals, the revolution in customs. Then there came the great boom. Conservatism, normal events, commonplace undertakings lost their appeal. It was the era of great stunts, of great and quick riches, of eager grabbing after easy wealth. No wonder appetites became spoiled or even perverted.

Once in a fine restaurant in New Orleans I saw a trivial incident which illustrates the point. It is well known that America has no finer chefs than some in New Orleans. Cooking, there, is an art, chefs are artists. Into this restaurant there came another man. He ordered the dishes for which the restaurant was famous, waited impatiently for the food to come on, and then when it was spread beautifully before him with all the grace and elegance possible, and with stirring aromas rising from the dishes, he called for pepper, salt, sauces of various kinds, and without even tasting the food proceeded to spice it up. The best of cooking, it seems, was not good for him. His sense of taste had been dulled to the delicious. He had so accustomed himself to hot seasonings that properly prepared food was not palatable to him.

It was, as I said, a trivial thing, but illustrative of our appetites in many of their phases. Hot seasonings, that's what we have become accustomed to. Therefore my friend of the dressing-room said that normal news was not fit to read.

Within the past six months I have analyzed the front pages of scores of newspapers, and many showed a preponderance of unhappy news. Out of twenty items on one front page, nine dealt with crime, four with bad business news, and the rest were miscellaneous—a divorce, a prohibition discussion, and so on. This page fairly represents other front pages, and I must conclude that it fairly represents what the readers demand, because in all this wonderful world of ours there is bound to be enough good news to fill at least half a front page. If we, the readers, preferred good to bad news, we'd get more of it. Once I talked with an editor and he told me unhappy events were news because they were unusual, that the usual is not news, hence he printed the unhappy events. Again I talked with him, and this time he said he printed bad news because there was so much of it.

"You mean it is usual?"

"Very much so."

"According to your own theory, then, you should now devote your pages to good news, which you imply has become unusual."

He laughed and said that I did not know the problems of the press and, in fact, I do not. But I do know that there are merchants who have prospered in the course of the depression. Now and then, over on an inside page, I have found that some company is maintaining its dividend rate. Why isn't that just as much news as if the company had discontinued? I believe the world is now ready, even hungry, for something stimulating, something constructive. Not for any return to those false predictions of bonanza times around the corner, not for any recurrence of propaganda organized by groups for their own benefit. But for a return to good normal interests.

I know of an old lady who divided her income into nine equal parts, keeping one for herself, with the other eight helping to support eight families, all strangers to her. Many persons are doing similar things. Indeed, I know of no one who has anything who is not sharing with others. Unemployment is news, and must be handled, but is it not also interesting that so many millions of people are acting generously? All governments have tried, in one way or another, to help those who are suffering, but what the governments have done is very little compared with what individuals have done and are doing. It is the fineness of individuals, it is the return to self-sacrifice, to unselfishness, to warm sympathy that has saved this land from very terrible conditions.

With this spirit of cooperation, this willingness to share, again fully awake in the land, there is no reason to believe that decadence has set in. Just the contrary. It is revival, not decadence, that is before us.

Chapter III

DID WE HAVE IT COMING TO US?

Somewhere between 1920 and 1930 God became unnecessary to a great many people. Men were making vast sums of money without really working for it. Their sense of personal power increased. Their vanity grew amazingly. Self-sufficient they were, with a somewhat indulgent attitude toward religion and God. Perhaps, after all, He should be endowed. They would take the matter up as soon as their pressing business engagements permitted. Nothing, of course, could interfere with business.

The "getting habit" had the country in those days. Prices rose out of proportion to values. Everything was inflated, but the ego of man was inflated more than anything else. Next came the inflation of his desires for things that were not essential, and for more of the essential items than were actually necessary. No one was thinking much about giving the other fellow as much as possible for his money; the idea was to get as much of his money as possible. Snobbishness, or "snootiness," entered business and was thought by many to be an asset.

I wonder if, in years to come, we shall not think and speak of those boom years as the Era of Folly? For it was that, despite the many good things it gave to us. But the spirit of folly was so pervading that it swept up men in all walks of life. The "new economics" said there was no upward limit to prosperity, that every man could *get* enough to make him rich. Poverty, many predicted, was a thing of the past. There was even some question as to the future of hard work. Perhaps that could be dispensed with! If everybody only would spend enough, everybody would have enough and to spare. So they told us.

Those years were made to order for fads, quick selling, speculation. The philosophy of extravagance gained momentum daily, and statisticians appeared with figures to prove that it all was permanent. The old standards were old-fashioned. New values had come to stay, and to keep on rising. Salesmen, henceforth, would merely have to take orders, not win them. Thrift, that ancient virtue which played such a great part in the making of America, was thrown into the discard. It was a time of self-indulgence.

"When you look back upon those boom days," I asked a friend, "what do you think of?"

"Of what a fool I was!" he answered.

I recall a boast made by one of our national figures of a few years ago. He was speaking of the scrap heaps to be seen outside every American city. We threw enough stuff away, he said, to make it absolutely certain that production would have to continue at its terrific rate, and even increase.

Think of boasting about wastefulness! I doubt if anything permanent ever has been built on prodigality. Intelligent spending, intelligent replacement of equipment, generosity, they accomplish worth-while progress. But not reckless waste.

One acquaintance of mine told me that he had his secretary buy for him every four months a dozen new shirts. That would be thirty-six shirts a year.

"What do you do with them?" I asked.

"Throw them out, or pack them away somewhere. I can't be bothered with examining cuffs to see whether they are fraying."

Another acquaintance who had a fine

home in the suburbs maintained, also, a place in the city where he had a duplicate equipment of clothing. Always he had his bags packed with fresh clothes in order that he might get away on a business trip at any time without preparation. Many business men did things of similar nature.

When you went into a shoe store the clerk assumed, or pretended to assume, that you had come for two pairs or maybe three or four pairs of shoes. It was not thought enough to sell just one pair at a time. In the clothing stores the assumption, or pretended assumption, was that you had come for at least two suits.

"Only one suit to-day?" the clerk would ask. "I think you'll want this pattern in both single and double-breasted, and surely you'll want a gray suit to alternate with the blue you have selected."

Somehow, a great many tailors seemed to

have hit on seven as the minimum number of suits a man could get along with. Why seven I never learned, but that was the number most often quoted to me. And hotel clerks, in those easy days, turned away as you approached the desk and either became quite busy elsewhere, or pretended to become so. There was a lot of "high-hatticism" about.

A friend of mine went into an automobile agency to buy a car.

"Now let's see," began the salesman. "What kind of car do you wish?"

"A passenger car," answered my somewhat naïve friend.

"Oh, yes, of course. But do you wish a car in which you may ride to the station (this friend was a commuter), one for your wife to go shopping in, or a pleasure car for week-ends and special outings? Football games, you know, and that kind of thing."

"Are you selling 'em now like women's

dresses, a special design for every occasion?"

"Well, of course you'll not care to use one car for all kinds of errands."

"Oh, yes, I will," said my friend. "What I'm looking for is a car for my own use in getting to and from the station, for my wife to go shopping in, my children to play in, that will do for the week-end, the middle of the week, for ordinary and special occasions, for baseball, football or anything else. And if you've got one with a lawn-mower attached I might like that. Can you fix me up?"

"Yes, sir, except for the lawn-mower," said the salesman, breaking into a laugh. Probably he had known all the time that his patter was not very convincing, but it was in keeping with his instructions, and if people fell for it, that was not his affair.

It was considered almost vulgar, you remember, to lift the hood of a car in those days and look under it. To do so might imply that you were interested in performance rather than in style.

There is no escaping the conclusion that there was a lot of silliness in "those good old days" of a few years gone. And some immorality, too, for it was an era of gambling, a time when old folk, or even conservative folk, were thought a little annoying. I was shocked once to hear a big executive say that he wished some plan might be devised whereby he could be rid of all employees over fifty. And still more shocked at what a friend of mine told me. He was helping to support some aged relatives, and went to a banker to work out the best possible plan.

"I think you are very unwise to think so much of these old folks," said this adviser. "They have to live, I know, but money you give to them is not well invested. There can be no return on it. Give it to your youngsters, and there will be social returns for fifty years."

Cold reasoning might approve that idea, but the heart can not. An era that would slight the aged, can not be regarded as very desirable, morally. I often think the heart a more dependable guide, in morals, than the head. Or probably they are coordinate guides. Only those actions should be taken that meet with the approval of both.

The crash came, of course. A crash always follows any artificial boom. We had forgotten that, forgotten it so universally that not yet have I met any man who can in honesty say, "I told you so. I knew it was coming." Immediately after the crash we bent our energies not toward adapting ourselves to change, but toward denying it. Hundreds, thousands of statements were issued, all of them designed to disprove the reality of what had happened.

Charts by the score were prepared. They showed that the "curve" soon would start upward again. It was hard, mighty hard, to cut free from those days of easy gains, lavish spending, sports galore, anticipations of a future devoid of toil. Was it possible that we would have to make adjustments?

Slowly the facts of the situation were accepted. After that they were exaggerated. We had been spending too much, now we are spending too little. We had been overconfident. Now we are too scared. When I began writing this chapter I went out to see a number of the sanest business men I know, and to each one I put this question:

"What one thing is hindering recovery today more than any other thing?"

"That's easy," answered the first. "The public is scared stiff."

Said the second: "People have lost faith in their own ability."

The third: "A lot of people seem to think that America is going out of business."

The fourth: "Lack of confidence in anything or anybody."

All of these answers come to the same thing. Fear now is our handicap. Let's think about that a while. Human needs can not pass away. America is not going out of business. Every one of us has all the ability, the ingenuity, the energy we had formerly, and more experience. Intellect has not suddenly curled up. Ambition, though somewhat quiet, is latent in every man, woman and child. Conditions are bad, yes. There are suffering, inconvenience, unemployment. Millions who are innocent of having created this mess, are victims of it. But is there any reason under the sun why we should give up? Is there any reason why we should invite certain defeat instead of striving for probable victory? All of us have been shaken down now. The inflation, even of the ego, is long since past. It's deflation we are contending with to-day; deflation as extreme as inflation ever was. In between these two extremes lies the common-sense course. I think we are ready to travel it.

That friend of mine who had been buying three dozen shirts a year discovered, at the outbreak of the depression, that his wife had been storing shirts away.

"I have enough to last me three years," he said to me back in 1929. Well, the three years are over.

In the early days of our commercial trouble nearly every one overlooked the fact that personal inventories were large. That is, most of us had more stuff than we actually needed. That was an invisible surplus. But it has been digested. I have been asking man after man whether he needs anything now, and every one says that he does.

Most of them are able to buy, too, but are holding back because of uncertainty, because of fear. Mass thinking works that way. It becomes excited, extravagant; then it becomes cautious, afraid. Now is the time for it to change again, returning to normal functioning. I am convinced of that. There is too much defensive, not enough offensive, effort to-day. Defense is wise, but battles are won by offense. What if there is a little risk in attacking? It is safer than remaining inactive. It is more sportsmanlike, too. If we are going to fail, let's fail trying to succeed!

In my rounds selling life insurance I meet with scores of important men. Often they astonish me by their acceptance of defeat.

"I can't talk with you to-day," said one of them. "I'm too worried."

"Will you be worried all day?" I asked.

"Yes, all the week, all the year."

That gave me an idea. It came to me after I had left his office, so I made another appointment and went back.

"I have a plan," I said, "to save your business from the doldrums into which you say it has drifted." (I might have said, and with truth, into the doldrums where he had steered it.)

"What, another plan?" asked this man. "I hear nothing but plans, plans, plans. From Washington, from financiers, from preachers, from professors, from Europe. And now here's one from a life insurance agent! What is it, you want me to buy a million-dollar policy, make my business the beneficiary and then fall into the river?"

"Nothing like that," I answered. "I want you to get out of deep water, not into it."

"Tell me how."

"You said you were too worried to think, too worried to act, too worried to eat, and that you expected to stay that way for at least a year."

"I guess I said something like that. Anyway, it's a fact."

"Has worrying done you any good? Has it increased your strength, sharpened your wits?"

"No."

"Has it hurt you as an executive?"

"I suppose so, but I can't stop it."

"I'm not even proposing that you stop it," I went on. "But you are a very efficient man, with a time for everything. A time to read your mail, a time to dictate answers, a time for seeing callers, a time for arranging finances, a time for conferences with your associates. Now, I suggest that you have a regular time for worrying."

"Say, what are you talking about?"

"About worrying," I answered. "You say you can not stop it. All right then, we'll say it is a part of the necessary routine of your business day. My plan is for you, and for all other worried business men, to set aside a part of each business day for worrying. Would an hour be enough time for it?"

"Either you are crazy or I am. Go ahead."

"I think perhaps an hour would be enough. Therefore I suggest that you send to each department head a memorandum announcing that you have decided to institute a worrying hour. Instruct each one to come to the conference room at a certain hour prepared to do all his worrying for that day. I think it would be well to have this worry period from eight until nine each morning, and so get it done and over with before work actually starts. But be sure that every man comes in the proper state of mind. He must bring with him his fears, doubts, grouches, disappointments, describe each and then give himself over to unqualified worrying for an hour."

"You think that would do any good?"

"I think it would, yes."

And I do think so. If I had a business of my own, and if my associates were worryers, I'd appoint a worrying hour. I'd send around some such notice as this:

"To the heads of all departments:

"I have become convinced that you are doing your worrying in a very unsatisfactory way. You appear to be scattering it out over the entire business day, fitting it in here and there, and often letting ordinary duties interfere with it. This business must be conducted in a manner as orderly and efficiently as possible. The beginning of orderliness and of efficiency is in our thinking; therefore I have decided upon a new policy designed to help us to arrange our thought processes. You are requested to meet with me each morning at eight o'clock, and from that hour until nine you are to do all your worrying for the day. Please be prompt, be gloomy, and bring with you as many fears, as many items of depressing news and as many sad predictions as possible.

(Signed) "Vash Young,
"President."

Now, honestly, would not some such policy as this be a good thing in business and in the home? I have always contended, you know, that if we humans were ordered to worry, ordered to handicap ourselves by forming hurtful mental habits, we would refuse. If that is true, my worry hour would result in a revolution against worry. In any event, it would help a man get rid of his woes all at once. I'm strong for it!

DID WE HAVE IT COMING TO US?

Some years ago I wrote a magazine article called *I Got Tired of Being a Fool,* and last year I wrote a book called *A Fortune to Share.* In these I told how I wasted twenty years in foolish living, in worrying, drinking, getting nowhere. Suddenly there came to me the realization that certain qualities are dominant. Love, sympathy, kindness, courage and the like. These qualities are bound to be stronger than the destructive elements in life, such as fear, greed, hate, worry and so on. If the beautiful qualities were not dominant life would have degenerated. It seemed to me, therefore, that the Divine Being, the center of life, must possess these dominant attributes and that I, made in His image, would be able to reflect them in my conduct. Yes, quite clearly I could do that if I tried hard enough, and it was my plain duty to do it. Thereupon, and at once, I resigned the position I had, stopped smoking, drinking, stopped coffee, tea and everything else I thought not good for me, and struck out on the greatest romance one can have, the romance of trying to model a life on the Divine Plan.

This Plan has made me an unqualified optimist, the happiest person in the world. I try never to think of myself as Vash Young, but to think of Vash Young as a bundle of constructive qualities to be expressed. Therefore, when I go out to make business calls I am not thinking first of the profit which might come to me, but of my ability and my duty to reflect in my conduct those attributes which I believe are Divine. I will not permit myself to be disappointed, for that is destructive. I never permit envy of a successful competitor to mar my happiness. To be true to my own Golden Standard, I must exercise at all times complete dominion over unhappiness from whatever cause.

Instead of putting the personal pronoun *I* over a hunk of flesh and blood and bones standing so high and weighing so many pounds, I like to put that pronoun over the most enduring qualities I can discover, and let those qualities shape my life. I swore off from being an agitated human being, waiting around for future events to happen in sufficient abundance to make me happy. Very quickly I became happy in claiming, then in possessing, permanent spiritual values.

Soon after I started out on this great adventure I found people bringing their troubles to me. Since that magazine article appeared and since my book was published, a great many persons have come or have written, asking, in substance, how they can cease to make fools of themselves. The answer is very simple: list the attributes of God and set out determined to reflect them in everything you do.

Down in Texas last year I was scheduled to make a talk on the subject "A Fortune to Share." Just before the time came for me to speak I saw a very ancient man come into the room, and with the aid of his walking stick he made his way down the aisle. He looked to be a hundred years old.

"Where's that fellow who got tired of being a fool?" he asked.

"I'm the man," I answered, going forward to meet him.

"Well, mister," he said, "I'm mighty glad to meet you, and I wish I'd 'a' met you a long time ago. I'm terrible tired of bein' a fool, and I've been one all my life."

Funny, perhaps, on the surface, but tragic underneath. What a pity he did not come to his senses seventy-five years ago! No man need be a fool. You may have made bad investments. You may make them again. You may have been deceived by the boom, like every one else. But such things are not of prime importance. The foolishness that hurts is that which goes on in the inner man. The folly of a few years ago was within us, not outside. The wild speculation, the greed for quick money, the demand for old folk to step aside, the cruel killing speed of those days—all this was inside us. Is not that, in itself, evidence that we permitted wrong values to take hold of us? It appears to me that our failure was first moral, then financial. Our recovery must be first moral, and then financial.

Chapter IV

THE ADVENTURE OF COMING BACK

I DOUBT if I can ever feel again the same thrill I felt when, about twelve years ago, I turned away from a path of disintegration and began a new life. I had thought I was about through, except for a plodding unhappy existence. My friends thought I could not do any better than I had done, and probably would do worse. I had no religion, no bravery and not much hope. I was not strong physically because I squandered my strength in foolish habits. Just making a living that was all. Doing nothing for anybody except myself and my immediate family, and not much for us. In those days I was like certain trained fleas I have seen.

Did you ever attend a flea circus? I am told that these funny little insects are not hard to train. For instance, they are put into a container with a lid on it. At first they jump and jump, hitting that lid every time and falling back to the floor of the container, but after a time they learn to jump just short of the lid. When the "professor" sees that they no longer hit the lid, he knows he has them trained to jump the height he wishes them to and no higher. It is then perfectly safe to remove the lid, for the fleas, having bumped their heads a million times, never again will leap higher than just short of the height of that lid.

Now, it seems to me that a whole lot of us human beings are like those fleas. We try to rise, meet an obstacle and fall back. Again we try, bump our heads and fall back, and finally we decide to try no more. It was so with me. I thought I had found my level. But there came to me a great awakening. I vowed to myself then and there that I would live happily and usefully. To make the break from my old life complete, I resigned the job I had and started out with about one hundred dollars and nothing to do. Nothing to do? Well, hardly! I had more to do than ever before or since, for I had on my hands the greatest fight in the world, the fight for dominion over my own weaknesses, the fight for self-control, the fight to replace destructive with constructive thinking. I won that fight, thanks to God, and the victory gave me a thrill that still causes me almost to shout with joy whenever I think of it.

That was my come-back. It has brought me unmeasured happiness. I can, therefore, recommend a come-back as one of the greatest adventures, one of the highest romances man can know. You can see, all around you, the stirring quality of a regeneration, a come-back. Go to a baseball game and watch a former star trying to regain his old-time cunning. The crowd will be with him, no matter whether he is playing on the home lot or away from home. Pause as you walk down the streets of your town and watch the expression on people's faces as they see some fellow townsman who has been very ill and now again is able to be about. There is a spirit of jubilation manifest.

Within the past few years I have spoken in nearly every state in the Union, and almost always some one of my hosts tells me the story of a come-back.

"See that man over there?" some one will say to me. "A year ago he was in a bad way. His business was on the rocks, and it looked as if he would have to give up. But he made the finest fight I ever saw, and now he is on his feet. It's men like that who make this town a good place to do business in."

I think the Salvation Army hit on the perfect slogan when they began telling us, some years ago, that "a man may be down but he's never out." That's a fact, for in the human heart there burns, always, a spark that can be fanned into flaming action. Every one of us knows somebody who has been down, and then has risen again. Here's a story told to me by a reporter:

His work, when he was a kid just out of college, was on a small-town daily, of which he became city editor. In his paper one morning there appeared the name of a man arrested the night before for drunkenness. The city editor never before had heard of that man, nor did he expect ever to see him. But that night, late, as he was pounding away on his typewriter a bedraggled stranger came into the office and walked over to the boy's desk. In his hand he held a crumpled and soiled copy of the morning's newspaper.

"What is it?" the city editor asked.

"See that name?" asked the seedy stranger, pointing with a dirty finger to the name of the man who had been arrested while drunk.

"Sure. What of it?"

"That's my name," said the man.

The editor started to rise, thinking a fight was on hand, but he settled back in his chair when he saw the expression on the visitor's face.

"Young man," said the stranger, "I'm a bum. A drunken bum. I've tried every cure for liquor, and not one of them is worth a cent. Liquor's got me, that's all. But young man, listen. I'm not asking for anything for myself, but I have a daughter, as decent a girl as ever lived. It nearly kills her when my name gets into the paper like this. Now I ask you for her sake, for God's sake, never print my name again unless I do something that's decent, which I never will!"

The shabby stranger broke down and sobbed on the boy's desk. Then he got up jerkily and went out the door. For a long time the editor sat and thought. Then he typed a notice, such as is stuck on the walls and partitions of most newspaper offices. "To all reporters and proof-readers," read the notice. "Hereafter the name —— is not to be printed in this newspaper unless some major event requires it, or unless the man himself can be made to appear in a favorable light."

This bum was entitled, my friend told me, to the same protection his newspaper proprietor gave the "reputable" and "distinguished" drunks of the community.

It was two years later before the name of the poor old sot came again to the attention of my friend.

Could it be possible that he had been awarded that contract? A drunken bum entrusted with putting up a building of such size? The city editor went out to see for himself what was what, and soon he located the stranger who had called on him one night two years before. And stranger is the right word, for this man was not at all like the old drunk.

"What happened?" asked the astonished reporter.

"I'll swear I don't know," answered the regenerated man. "It came about in the course of one night. I decided all of a sudden that I'd not die a hog's death, that I'd be a man for a little while, anyway. The rest was easy, for when I won the mental fight, when I once swore off without any strings tied to my resolution to stop drinking, I just stopped."

Now that *was* a come-back!

But every town has such stories. What we need now is a great collective come-back, a return to honesty of effort and of thinking, a return to courage. In other words, we need to make the best instead of the worst of the situation we are in. For several years I have been meeting, from time to time, a man who has enjoyed a big income. He has been pretty well cleaned out lately, however, and the loss of his money almost killed him. It was very disappointing to those of us who had admired him to see his inability to stand up under this loss.

"But listen," he said to me, "can't you understand what a fix I'm in? I tell you I haven't ten thousand dollars to my name."

"Have you got a thousand?" I asked.

"Oh, certainly, I have that much."

"Well, you have more than the average person in this country if you have a thousand dollars in the bank. Do you consider that you are deserving of more than the average run of mankind?"

"No, I suppose not, but it's hard . . ."

"Yes, I know it's hard to lose money. But it would be harder, wouldn't it, to lose your wife or any one of three fine children?"

"Don't be silly."

"I'm not being silly. You are the silly one. Here you are with health, a wonderful family, and several thousand dollars more than the average man, yet you are worrying yourself crazy. Come here," I urged, "let's go out there and ask that truck driver if he has a thousand dollars."

My friend did not wish to come, but I dragged him to the curb and explained to the truck driver that we were not crazy, but were making a sort of financial test.

"Have you a thousand dollars in the bank?" I asked him.

"Heck, no!" he said. "Who do you think I am, Rockefeller?"

Things are relative, you see. That truck driver would have considered a thousand dollars in cash a fortune; my friend thought disaster had come upon him because he had only about ten thousand.

"Now, I have a suggestion to make to you," I said to my friend. "I want you to take stock of yourself. Put down your real assets on a piece of paper, and on another write down all the harassing things that are cluttering up your mind."

Together we worked out the lists, and found, of course, that in the real things of life this man was rich.

"If I were you," I said, "I'd take this other list in a big envelope and check it each morning when I came into the Grand Central Station. Yes, sir, go to the parcel-room and check my envelope in which I had set down worry, fear and all that kind of destructive junk."

He would not quite do that, but he got the point none the less.

I doubt if any depression could survive a concerted come-back effort of more than a hundred million people. Not an artificial effort, worked up by interested persons or organizations for their own good, but an earnest determination on the part of every man, woman and child to banish fear, worry and greed, and to replace them with courage, cheer and unselfishness. The come-back we need is a return to a true sense of values, an eagerness to attain the great prizes of life, not just eagerness for the great payments in money. A long time ago I made my own list of prizes worth striving for. This list

I keep before me in order that I may check and recheck my conduct and my attainments by it. For your own purposes, you can make a better list than mine, because you, and you alone, know what are the great prizes for you. Anyway, here is my list:

1. Unselfishness. So long as I think much of myself, I will not be worth much to others, and thoughts of self are invitations to trouble.

2. Fearlessness. I do not know of any good thing ever erected upon the foundation of fear. It is fear that causes one country to arm against another; therefore it is fear that brings on war. Fear, in individuals and in nations, produces the very things of which men are afraid.

3. A good standing at home. It is easy to show to advantage away from home, but the acid test of disposition and of character comes when I am under my own roof. If

I am a failure there, I am, indeed, a failure and should begin at once to bring on my come-back.

4. Honesty. Not just the kind that keeps me from stealing; but rather the kind that makes me realize that my time and attention belong to the task in hand. If I am working for another man I should, in business hours, work for him and not think of my own troubles and my own desires. Business honesty is a virtue much too rare. I must be safe by giving more than I am supposed to give, either to my customers, my employers or my employees. No man can afford to take chances with honesty, lest he destroy his own happiness.

5. Patience. Patience in the home, in business. Patience on the golf course, on the highways, at tennis, in bridge—patience everywhere. Some one has defined a moron as an automobile driver who thinks that by

blowing his horn he can start the stalled motor ahead of him. It is a good definition. I often wonder why people go to ride, for they seem to keep themselves in a stew all the time. They swear at all other drivers, hold their lips in ugly snarls, get furious when a man ahead stops to make a left-hand turn and assume that he is stopping just for dumbness. I believe, taken all in all, mankind shows up worse behind a steering wheel than anywhere else in the world. Patience on the road. What a blessing that would be!

6. Poise. Every one envies the man or woman who has it. No one admires excitability, lack of control, high tremulous speaking. Poise as a preventive of nervousness, and as a business asset, is worth my trying for.

7. Tolerance. What a silly thing it is to condemn some one else because he does not agree with me! Looking at it another way,

I do not agree with him. I pray constantly that I may grow in tolerance. If some one makes a mistake, I must not be too quick to condemn. But if some one does a thing well, I must be quick to praise. I have known men—too many of them—who consider their functions as executives require them to be mean, but the executive who is generous with his praise gets more work out of his associates than the surly boss. And tolerance is, to me, close to the heart of religion.

8. Thrift. It is a real joy to be thrifty. Not stingy, but saving of effort, of money, of things about the house.

9. Justice. Justice in mind and in deed. Fairness in my divisions with others. Be sure that no advantage is taken of a less fortunate person. Because a man is out of work and desperately in need is no excuse for beating him down to the lowest possible

figure. I must be sure that I'm just, or my own inner integrity will be in jeopardy.

I believe you would find it a high adventure to make your own list of great prizes, and then strive to attain each one. I am sure, if you do this, you will forget a whole lot of your business worries, and once they are forgotten, things will begin to improve. It looks to me as if these next few years can be made into a great Era of Sanity, as contrasted with the Era of Folly out of which we now are emerging.

Chapter V

HOW TO GET UP IN THE MORNING

In sales conventions, in conferences and elsewhere I have heard hundreds of persons say that the most important part of any task is the completion of it. I know what they mean. I know what they want—orders. But I wonder if they are correct? Obviously, if you do not start, you can not finish. If you do not start well, do you often finish successfully? When I set out to remake my own life, I decided that, so far as I was concerned, the most important part of every action is the start of it. I would, therefore, be certain I was in the best possible state of mind, that I had the best possible presentation of my subject prepared, and that I had given full consideration to the needs, the temperament and the financial situation of my client before I called to see him.

I kept working back and back in my thinking until finally I came to see that my first task, each day, was to begin that day intelligently. It could not be a complete success if the start was a failure, and partial success was not my goal. I wished complete success as far as my own performances could be judged. I do not mean that I hoped for success in every business venture. Not that, at all. Again, it was the inner man I was thinking of. That Golden Standard of my own which I have mentioned.

For years I had been awaking each morning with a bad taste in my mouth, and with such disagreeable feelings that I actually could not tell, until ten or eleven o'clock in the forenoon, whether or not I was sick. My body did not function well, my mind functioned worse and my disposition was awful. Why? The fault, surely, was my own. Nature never fashioned any such imperfect thing as my body was in those days. Children are irrepressible in the mornings. Birds do their finest singing and their hardest work in the mornings. Animals are refreshed at the start of every day. Why then should man, supposed to be nature's masterpiece, be a sour failure until the day is half spent? Why then should one particular man—myself—be such a failure?

"The first victory I must win each day," I said to myself, "is against the obstacles which I first meet. Those obstacles are of my own fashioning. I'll get rid of them."

It was then that I cut out tobacco, whisky, coffee, tea, late hours, over-eating, worrying, envy and everything else I could hit on as being an enemy to perfect performance by the inner man. It was a strenuous campaign, marked by some sharp fighting, but I won it, and ever since I have felt in perfect form when I first wake up. I made it a practise to do something for somebody immediately on arising. It is splendid discipline. More than that, it is splendid common sense, for when a day is well begun, it is likely to continue smoothly.

I have talked with dozens of men and women about this, and have found that almost without exception they are below par, below their best when they first get up. Some must have cigarettes, others coffee, others must get out and away from home before they begin to approach normal. There is no sense in that. The ante-breakfast and the post-breakfast grouches are without excuse.

"You never had to take care of a sleepless baby," said one woman to me.

"That's a fact," I agreed. "But does it

make matters better for you to be glum in the mornings?"

"If you felt as mean as I do in the mornings," said a man, "you'd think you had won a victory when you refrained from hitting somebody."

"Why do you feel so mean?"

"I don't know. I guess it's natural."

With that I certainly could not agree. It positively is not natural. No grouch is natural. It is the result of foolishness somewhere, of uncontrolled appetites, or too little sleep, of too little philosophy, of too little thoughtfulness of others. The penalties for self-indulgence, whether in appetites or in disposition, are too heavy. No man in his right mind should pay a hundred times more than a thing is worth. A little over-indulgence in midnight food, in smoking, in drinking may bring a sort of temporary pleasure, but also it brings discontent that lasts ten or even a hundred times longer than the pleasure did. In happiness I'm a bargain hunter. I want a whole lot of it at the least possible cost, and I have been able to get it too. The cost was no more than self-control. It demanded merely that I replace destructive habits and emotions with those that are constructive. Never in my life have I found a greater bargain than when I started over again in my thinking and in my outward conduct. I hesitate to make any statement too general; therefore I am reluctant to say, for certain, that what was good for me would be good for all. Yet I have all the appearance and the equipment of the average man, and no more. It may be, therefore, that what is possible and profitable for me, would be the same for many others. Anyway, I wish some would try it, for I know I am happy, and I want every one else to be.

At best, the grouchy man is funny; at worst, he is destructive of his own happiness and that of others. Obviously, he should do something about his testy moods, but too frequently his attitude is that of the man who suffered with bunions, and who made his sufferings very vocal.

"If you have bunions," suggested a friend, "why don't you do something for them?"

"Why should I?" asked the grouch. "They have never done anything for me!"

In the mornings the earth is clean, the air is pure. A new day is handed to me to do with as I will. I am thankful for it, and for the possibilities which it brings. Often I think it would be better for those who pray in the morning, to thank God for blessings already received instead of asking for more. Thankfulness is very close to happiness. Rarely are thankless persons happy.

A wealthy old lady in New York has for eight years been giving a hundred dollars a month to an acquaintance of hers, another woman. There is no obligation between the two. The money is paid merely because the old lady wishes to do as much good as she can. Once recently the check was two or three days late, and the beneficiary telephoned to the benefactor's secretary and in the nastiest sort of way denounced her for being careless in sending out the check.

"I had planned to go off," she said hotly, "and your carelessness has made it necessary for me to postpone the trip."

"The check is in the mail now," said the secretary.

"It should have been in the mail three days ago," retorted the woman.

The wealthy old lady's secretary became angry, and justly so. She spoke to her employer and suggested that the check be omitted the next month just to teach the other woman a lesson.

"Oh, no," said the old lady. "She is so unhappy, anyway."

Of course she is! An ungrateful person has almost no chance for happiness.

When I was a boy an old hobo settled in a little town where some acquaintances of mine lived. He had no more than other hobos, which means that he had nothing at all by way of material possessions. Yet he was a pretty good sort. People liked him because he was so cheerful. Every time he got a hand-out he beamed with gratitude. No one knew, or cared, where the old fellow slept. Every one supposed that somebody else took care of him at night. But one day he came into the store of a merchant, a man who had a farm on the edge of town.

"I'd like to speak to Mr. Smith," said he.

"What for?" asked a clerk. "Need a suit?"

"No, it ain't that. I want to thank him for somethin'."

Mr. Smith came out of his cage.

"Thank me?" he asked. "For what? I never gave you or any other hobo anything."

"Well, sir, I been sleepin' in your barn, and that hay you put in last week has got less briers in it than any you've cut in a long time. I can sleep fine now."

A little of that spirit among those of us who have not yet been, or ever will be, reduced to sleeping in the hay, would do a lot right now toward straightening out the mental mess we are in, even if not the financial. But, as I keep on saying, I believe that when the thinking gets right, other good things follow. I'm certain that right thinking in the morning has helped me to make a good living.

Now and then when people are telling me their troubles I ask them what are their first thoughts on awakening. The answers are amazing and amusing. One man told me he was too stupid, when he first awoke, to think of anything. Another said he wondered where he had left his cigarettes. A third confessed that the weather always seemed bad to him—it was going to be too hot, too cold, too wet or something. A fourth said it always struck him that his wife and children, in the morning, were trying deliberately to plague him. A salesman told me he awoke dreading the rounds he must make. A stock-broker said he could not eat breakfast until he had looked at the financial pages and learned the worst. . . . And so on.

All of these men are intelligent, or would be if they would give themselves half a chance. Their conduct, their untrained emotions, their undisciplined thoughts seem to me very unfortunate. I can see no excuse in physiology or in morality for bad temper in the mornings. Every person owes it to himself, his family and his employer to begin each day right. But what do we see in the great American home? Mothers fretting because children will not dress, children demanding to know where somebody hid their clothes, husbands hurrying through with bathing and shaving and then gulping breakfast. A veteran conductor on a commutation train said he rarely if ever had pulled out of a station without seeing some one making a futile dash for the train. Of those who make the train, said he, there always are some who have cut themselves in shaving, and others who still have soap in their ears. Now, what's the sense in hurrying like that? The human race is bound to have more intelligence than it shows in the mornings. Otherwise it would have been crowded off the face of the earth by animals that know when to go to bed, how to get up and what to eat.

Personally, I think it a fine thing to form the habit of thinking of others and doing something for others before beginning the day's work. There are scores of nice ways to begin a day. Writing notes to friends, for instance. I know one woman who keeps a "friendship note" calendar. Every date of any importance to her friends is on this calendar. Each morning she turns it ahead a few days to see if any anniversaries are due. If so, she writes notes of congratulation. In the course of a year she sends out more than two hundred notes and letters of this kind. Only ten minutes or perhaps fifteen are required for each one. Not many of us are so busy we could not squeeze in a little thought of somebody else before breakfast.

An advertising man told me he had used

his newsboy as his disposition trainer. The boy's stand was on the first corner outside this man's apartment-house, and usually he over-paid the boy.

"If I'm feeling pretty good," said the advertising man, "and do not need much discipline, I give the boy a nickel and leave the change with him. If I'm not feeling so good, I give him a dime. If I'm really low in my mind, I give him a quarter, and when I have felt downright rotten I have given him as much as fifty cents. I really do it for my own good. It helps put me in a decent frame of mind before I reach the office."

A moral analysis of this man's conduct is difficult, but the effect of it is good for him, good for the newsboy's income, and good for the people in the man's office.

I know another man who makes himself speak pleasantly to a number of persons each morning—the elevator boy, the doorman, the policeman on the corner.

"It does me good," he confesses.

Of course it does.

I have heard people say that no one can get decent attention in New York unless he pays for it, but this is not true. There have been times when I had no money for tips, but I never found people insulting. Pleasant manners go a long way anywhere. In return for them the bootblack puts on an extra lick or two, the elevator boy comes promptly at your signal, the doorman finds a taxi at once, the taxi driver proceeds with a little care over the bumps in the street, the Pullman porter tries to increase your comfort, the milk man makes less noise when he sets down the bottles if you have been decent to him—and so on through the contacts of life. Good manners mean consideration for others, consideration for others means less thought of self, less thought of self means less gloom, and less gloom means less depression.

Look at it any way you will, it pays to start the day right, and to continue it as you began.

Chapter VI

THE FIFTY-SECOND CALL

Selling is, for me, the most interesting work in the world. All my adult life I have been engaged in selling one thing or another. For a time it was newspaper space, then magazine space, and now it is life insurance. I do not know of any other occupation that requires so much self-control, so much optimism, or so continuous a fight against discouragement. It has been hard, these past few years to sell anything.

"And don't we know it!" a million salesmen say.

Yet, by changing my methods and increasing my efforts, I have been able to hold my own in the highly competitive field of insurance. Perhaps that is why I have been asked to address so many gatherings of salesmen.

From the platform and in person I have talked with thousands. I don't know how they liked it but *I* have enjoyed every single talk. I feel closer to salesmen than to any other group in the world. They speak my language and I speak theirs. I know what they are up against, and what they have been up against. A few years ago every salesman was driven faster and faster as one quota period ended and another began. Every firm in the country was raising its expectations every year, demanding a ten-, fifteen- or twenty-per-cent. increase over the sales of the preceding year. Obviously, that could not go on for ever. There is a limit to human consumption power. If the theory of the sales managers in 1928 had been correct, the world by now would have been cluttered with every sort of thing imaginable. The speed was too great, the rate of increase impossible as a permanent thing. But it was two or three years after the crash before the bosses would admit that anything had happened—that is, before they would admit the truth to the salesmen.

"There's plenty of business," said they, "if you'll only go and get it. The fault is with you, not with conditions."

That was untrue, artificial and often cruel. Now the feelings and the admissions have swung too far the other way. There is a sort of defeatism evident. I have been into several stores recently where the salesmen seemed to take it for granted that I did not intend to buy. They were courteous enough to me, but their attitude showed very plainly they are discouraged. So many persons have come in, looked around and then gone out with nothing bought that sales forces have come to expect it. That oldest of all customer bromides—"Well, I'll look around, and if I don't see something I like better I'll come back"—has been spoken billions of times in the course of this depression, and every salesman in America knows that when a customer says it, there is almost no chance that he will come back. It is simply an excuse where no excuse is needed. The air of dejection in stores is easy to understand but not so easy to condone. Thousands of sales are being missed because the sales folk do not try hard enough, or because they are not fitting their efforts in with the mind of the times.

A store salesman confided to me that he could not work effectively because he was in constant fear of losing his job.

"What's the matter?" I asked.

"Sales are falling off," he answered. "I'm doing only about half that I did last year."

"If I were in your situation," I suggested, "I think I'd increase instead of decrease my efforts. The fact that business is slow is the strangest reason I ever heard of for slackening in your efforts. Here you are about to lose your job because your sales are falling off, and your sales are falling off because you are afraid of losing your job! Why, man, you are creating the necessity for letting you out!"

Every man who now is holding a job has greater incentive than ever before to give it the best he has. In normal times perhaps a salesman can get by with less than his best, but in times of stress only the best of which we are capable is good enough. Now and then you see a man who has had a salary cut, and is angry over it. He makes up his mind that he will not put out as much effort in the future as he has in the past, because he is not being paid as much. What a silly attitude! The fact that a salary cut was necessary is in itself ample evidence that greater, not lesser, effort is required to maintain business.

No man can sit around in times such as we have been contending with and wait for others to create the demand for his retention in his post; he must take the initiative and create the demand himself.

Out on Long Island, New York, there is a chain-store clerk who did it. No doubt there are tens of thousands of others, but I happen to know of this one. He knew business was shaky, so he redoubled his efforts to please his customers. He would telephone to them when he had bargains, or when there was some especially choice food on hand. He waited upon them quickly and pleasantly. In every way, he became a better salesman than he had been, because he had the imagination to know that the times demanded better service. None the less, an order came through from somewhere to cut off a salesman, and this young fellow was chosen for the sacrifice. He was fired, transferred to something less desirable, or something of the kind. Anyway, he did not appear at his old stand. Customers asked about him, and then, without any planned "strike" by the women of the neighborhood, many of them simply stopped trading with that store. The manager dashed around to ask them what was wrong, and they told him! The result was inevitable—the popular salesman returned.

I see a great many men in the course of each week, and they represent all walks of life. I talk business with them, ask them how they feel about conditions, and all that kind of thing. Unless I am badly mistaken the public, if I can gage it by the men with whom I come into contact, is about ready to buy now. I have already said something about this and I want to say more. Now is the time to be alert, not downcast.

Said one man to me:

"I've been doing without things long enough. If the country goes broke my savings will be no good anyway, so I have decided to go out and get what I need."

There is some sportsmanship, some courage in that view-point, and I have an idea this man came very close to describing the state of mind of the country at large. A whole lot of people have been unable to buy anything, but the vast majority have had something to spare all along. It was fear, over-caution, doubt as to the future of America that has held them back. The mass mind was afraid, but the mass mind does not remain afraid for any great length of time. You have noticed, of course, how certain ideas gain almost universal currency all of a sudden, and for no apparent reason. I am convinced that the next great wave of feeling is going to sweep us into better times. America is not going to stay scared for ever. Everywhere I see crowds look into store windows. Some people say they are the unemployed, who are looking because they have nothing else to do. I doubt that. I believe most of them are employed, that they are looking at articles they want, and that pretty soon they'll be buying them.

The popular wish now is to buy, not to hold back. Something, I do not know what, will start the procession, and if I were a merchant I'd be all set to cash in on it. Everybody knows there are bargains everywhere. Our dollars will buy more than at any other time in many years. This chance for bargains can not last indefinitely, nor will our Yankee love for bargains lie dormant indefinitely.

For my own guidance I made a set of rules for these times. Perhaps some of them will help you. Anyway, here they are:

1. During working hours, either be in a prospect's office or on the way to one.

2. Remember, nearly every one has been hit and hit hard; therefore do not run the risk of embarrassing a prospect, or of losing a sale, by suggesting too much to him. Have a heart! It is better to offer a man less than he can buy, and let him raise it, than to offer him more and thus force him to cut you down. He feels good when he raises something to a higher figure, but a little uncomfortable when he must shave down.

3. Adjust the presentation to suit the times. Think in terms of my prospect's needs instead of my own.

4. Imagine myself in my prospect's shoes, and deal with him, always, as I should like a salesman to deal with me.

5. Never argue. Possibly I could win the argument, but almost certainly I'd lose the sale.

6. Be sincere. If I do not believe what I have to offer is good for a man in these times, I'll not call on him. Every sale in days such as these must be mutually beneficial. The artificiality of the boom is over. The law says, "Let the buyer beware," but this is not good enough ethics for the new start business must make.

7. Be cheerful, always. I'll not be cast down by a refusal. I'll salvage something out of every call I make. If no sale results, at least I shall have had an experience with an interesting person, for every person is interesting.

8. Be certain that I have a liberal number of tough prospects on my list. It's fine to land any order, but especially fine when a hard prospect is convinced. They give me

the chance to prove my ability as a salesman.

Those rules are for me in my own line, but now and then I show them to others. A clothing-store clerk, for example.

"But what would you do," he asked, "if you were selling clothes?"

"I'd proceed on the assumption that every customer was a Scot, looking for the greatest possible return for his money. I'd talk value, durability, low price to him."

"We did not do that back in 1928. Just the opposite, and those were the days when we had our biggest business."

"Yes, but the public attitude is just the opposite now of what it was in 1928. Selling must be based, always, on the attitude of the public. Selling methods can not be standardized."

Another man asked me if I actually enjoyed a tough prospect. The answer is yes.

The harder they are to sell, the more they interest me. For instance:

One of the most delightful adventures I ever had was with a man who put me off fifty-one times. First, I read an item about him in a trade paper and decided he would be a good man to know. I therefore wrote him a letter congratulating him on his new position described in the trade paper, and asked if I might come to see him. A few days later I telephoned to him and was delighted at his cordiality.

"This is going to be easy," I said to myself.

But he did not set a time for me to see him. He said he was going to Boston, or somewhere, and asked that I telephone to him again the next week. I did, and this time he was going to Philadelphia. Would I telephone again in a week? Of course, but the only result was another excuse.

Week after week this went on. I telephoned to him each Monday, and each Monday he had a fresh excuse for not seeing me. I accepted every excuse without question. We became well acquainted over the phone, though neither of us had the slightest idea what the other looked like.

After a whole year of this, and on my fifty-second call, he broke into a big laugh.

"Young," said he, "I have run out of excuses. Come on over and let's go to the mat on this thing."

I went at once and was received as an old friend.

"You are by all odds the most patient man in the world," said he.

"With one exception," I answered, "and you are it."

"Well, I feel guilty about all the time you have wasted on me. I'm not interested in insurance."

"It isn't very interesting, is it?"

"Why, I thought you were in the insurance business!"

"I am, but the interesting thing to me is not insurance, but the possibility of your having an income for life."

That got his attention. He had been thinking of some other form of insurance, and here I had suggested a kind he did not understand. He asked questions. I submitted to him an illustration of what I had in mind. He decided it would be a fine thing for him, raised my proposal and in the end I got his application for an annuity contract that called for an annual deposit by him of ten thousand dollars. Was that worth fifty-two calls? I think it was, and he thinks it was.

I have concluded that it is not the things a salesman *fails* to do that wreck him. Not a bit of it. He goes to pieces because of the things he *does* do. For instance, he provides himself with competition that is ruinous; competition, that is, which springs from within him and therefore cripples every effort he makes. A few years ago there were a great many novels written that gave us what I understand is known as "the stream of consciousness." They just set down the random thoughts of the characters. I wish somebody could set down the stream of consciousness of a salesman who is disgusted with his luck; one of those fellows who is providing his own competition. It would run something like this:

"I don't feel right this morning. . . . Monday is a bad day to see people anyhow. . . . Nobody's buying anything these days. . . . Might as well give us all a vacation. . . . The old man doesn't know what we are up against. . . . Wonder how I stand with him? . . . Gosh! he gives me all the tough eggs. . . . Maybe he's trying to make me quit. . . . I'd like to. . . . Made Bill manager in our territory when I'm a better salesman than he is every day in the week. . . . Guess I'll telephone to Harry and ask him what sort of week-end he had. . . . I'll plan a big day for to-morrow. . . . Wonder what my bank balance is? . . . Nothing, probably. . . . My wife went shopping while I was away. . . . Business is terrible. . . . Those bears down in Wall Street ought to be hamstrung and quartered. . . . Gosh! I'd like to pick up a little easy money in the market. . . . Not a chance. . . . Dropped everything I had on that tip Tom gave me. . . . Said he knew what he was talking about. . . . Crazy. . . . Say, wasn't that a poor shot I made on the ninth hole yesterday? . . . Caddie got me flustered by walking in my line of vision. . . . Where do they get those dumb caddies? . . .

Believe I've got indigestion. . . . Breakfast was terrible. . . . It does seem that a woman with nothing else to do could think up a decent breakfast for a fellow. . . . I'm sick of eggs. . . . Give me many more and I'll start cackling. . . . Wonder if that cut on Junior's foot will amount to anything? . . . Mary ought to have more sense than turn him out barefooted. . . . More doctor's bills and me broke. . . . I'm all out of prospects. . . . Wonder why the government doesn't do something. . . . We can't go on like this. . . . Lent a fellow five dollars last month and haven't seen him since. . . . Never will see him again, probably. . . . Say, I hate that guy they're bringing on here from the West. . . . So full o' pep he'll explode some day. . . . Oh, well, let him tackle my territory a while and he'll flop worse than I ever did. . . . Guess I'll go on out now and see what new excuses the customers have thought up over the week-end. . . . I don't blame 'em. . . . I wouldn't buy anything either in times like these."

And so on. How can a man who lets his mind roam around like that expect to do an honest day's work? Action is the only way to straighten out a mental mess of that sort. When you feel your thoughts getting scrambled, grab your hat and start somewhere. Cold canvassing is far better than dreaming away precious hours. More honest, too, for you are not paid to think of such things as I've just set down. Nor to spend your time wondering how you stand with the boss. The thing for you is not to be scared he will fire you, but to make him scared you will quit. The present is a testing time. Too many of us have been what a stage comedian describes as "independent salesmen." That is, salesmen who take orders from nobody. And one explanation is that we have gone out convinced that nothing good would come as a result of our efforts. The man who does not first sell his own idea to himself, is not likely to sell it elsewhere. Admitting defeat in advance is just no good at any time! Here's an incident which, of my own knowledge, is correct:

A woman went into a carpet store to buy some rugs. The weather was very hot, and the rug business, of course, is not very brisk in the midst of a hot summer. Still, she had her own reasons for wishing to buy at that time. Inside the store she saw no one to wait on her. She rapped on the counter, yet there was no response. Finally she walked far back into the room and there discovered the proprietor asleep on a pile of rugs. She hesitated to awaken him, so came on out. Of course she told of the incident. It was too funny to keep to herself. The proprietor's explanation made it even funnier.

"I just didn't believe anybody would come in on such a hot day to buy rugs," said he.

Do you know what really is the matter with a great many of us to-day? I do, for I have listened to hundreds talk, and I've listened to their wives,—hundreds who have been out of work, and other hundreds who have been demoted in one way or another. So many of these have come to see me that I prepared a characteristic conversation between a depressed man and his wife, and this I pass out to callers when they seem to need it. I think it illustrates why some men fail. Here it is:

RUTH: And now tell me all about it, Dick. Just to think! After all those months of discouragement, you've got a job at last.

DICK: Do you call this a job?

RUTH: Well, it isn't so good as some others you've had. But after all, you were a salesman with Murray & Williams—and you were a good salesman too, so you ought to be a good salesman to-day.

DICK: Yeah! That sounds all right. But just because Murray & Williams sent me such a good letter of recommendation, these people have given me their hardest prospects to sell.

RUTH: But, Dick,—that's the kind of prospects you used to love. I remember how you used to come home and tell me about the prospects you called "hard-boiled yeggs," and you used to say, "That bird wanted to kick me out of his office at first, but I stuck with him until I got his order."

DICK: Yes. That was all right then. But it's different these days. Besides, why should they make a salesman out of me? I've been a branch manager. Why should I go back to being a salesman?

RUTH: But, Dick,—after all it *is* a job,—and you haven't had a job for over a year.

DICK: A job! Call that a job! You can't sell anybody in these hard times. It's just a waste of time to call on them.

RUTH: How many did you call on today, Dick?

DICK: Well—I—well, I didn't actually make any calls. I looked over the list of prospects they gave me and I knew there wasn't one of them who would even let me into his office to talk to him.

RUTH: But what did you do all day?

DICK: Well, I—I sort of outlined the best way to go about it. I phoned and called on people I knew to see if I couldn't get personal introductions to any of these prospects.

RUTH: And did you find any?

DICK: No—I didn't. But I will.

RUTH: Well, why don't you just call on the prospects and see? Maybe some of them will talk to you. Maybe some of them want just what you've got to sell.

DICK: Aw, don't be foolish, Ruth. Nobody wants to buy anything these days. It's just no use, I tell you. Besides, how can you expect me to get interested in a job like this one? I'm ten times as good a branch manager as the one they've got. Let 'em give me a chance at that fellow's job and I'll show 'em something.

The woods are full of men who look at life as Dick does. Conditions have brought about all sorts of adjustments. Pride and false dignity have received some hard knocks. A time of testing, that's what we have been through. How have we met it? How do we intend to keep on meeting it? Every man has before him at all times the choice between certain defeat, which he can bring down on his own head, and probable victory, which he can achieve. This is what makes life such a grand romance!

Chapter VII

HOBBIES FOR PEOPLE WHO WORK

When people ask me how I manage to be so eagerly interested all the time, I tell them I have a hobby.

"What is it?" they ask.

"Living in successful rebellion against all the lost motion, grief, discontent and unhappiness I see around me."

Stated differently, my hobby is to be continuously happy. I can not be that unless I maintain steady dominion over my own thoughts and feelings. Victories that are won in the mind and in the heart are the basis of contentment.

"Suppose your work was uninteresting," one man asked, "what would you do then?"

"I'd make it interesting," I told him. "I'd transform it into a hobby, if necessary, or develop a hobby in connection with it."

I am convinced that can be done. I have talked with scores of persons who have done it. Right now I believe all of us could become happier by adopting as our hobby the determination to get out of the depression; make ourselves interested in every possible action designed for that end. The human being in times of depression is highly entertaining. The human being always is highly entertaining.

"I haven't been selling so much these past few years," said a salesman, "but I've had a good time trying. To keep myself interested I began to analyze and classify my prospects. My groupings include redheaded men, baldheaded men, fat men and lean men, married men and single men. I'm trying to figure out how members of these groups react to different situations. Every man I call on falls into one or more of my groups, and no matter how he acts, he either confirms or denies one of my theories. Married men, I have concluded, are more scared of hard times than single men. That's natural. Fat men are harder to sell in hot weather than in cold. That, too, seems natural. Red-headed men fight me off more quickly than others. Baldheaded men always are a little sensitive about their domes, and I've found it bad strategy to let them catch me glancing at their heads. Look into a baldheaded man's eyes, or at his clothes. . . . There are a lot of other things I've concluded, all of which may be right or wrong. It doesn't matter to me. I'm not a scientist. Only a salesman keeping himself interested."

A store clerk told me he had found it very entertaining to chart the conduct of the average customer. This clerk has found that almost no one comes in with his mind fully made up. If the customer is a man and wishes a pair of socks, he must be asked a number of questions. What size? What color? What price? Silk or lisle? Any special brand? Before the depression, he says, women had begun buying all sorts of items for their husbands, but now the men are getting back into shopping, and they are harder to sell than are women. When a woman is buying for her husband she is likely to get the best she possibly can afford, but when he is buying for himself he likes to find bargains. Men now are proud of how little they pay for stuff, and they boast of the age of their clothes. But not women! Back in boom days women were spending nearly all the money spent in America. That isn't so true now.

"I have a lot of fun," says this clerk, "sizing up my customers, listening to their excuses when they do not buy, noting the changes in their attitude as the depression progresses. This gives me something to think about in the course of the day, and something to talk about when I go home in the evening. My wife nearly always asks me if I had any interesting contacts in the store; usually I have a story or two for her."

That strikes me as a pretty good hobby. This man is learning about people, which means that he is making himself a better salesman all the time, and also he is making himself a more entertaining husband.

I have been tempted to make a "collection" of hobbies. Many of them are fascinating. In one of those lovely New England villages with a large green in the middle of it, a man has been employed for years to keep the grass cut in summer, the leaves raked in autumn and the snow shoveled back in winter.

"It's the grass cutting I like best," he says. "I keep track of the number of miles I walk in a day behind the mower. I figure now that I've done better than fifty thousand miles on this one green. I know the date when the first cutting is due in spring, and the last in the fall. Sometimes we have a late spring, sometimes an early one. It means something to me—less mileage or more mileage in the course of the summer. Maybe this looks silly to you, but it's my job to cut grass, and I might as well get some fun out of it if I can."

He's everlastingly right! We need more fun in this life, and I respect any man who has discovered ways to get it out of his work. Over in New Jersey I have time and again watched a boy cutting his father's lawn. I doubt if he likes the task, for grass cutting isn't in itself exciting. But this boy works out mathematical designs in his cutting.

That is, he does not begin at one edge and work over, but he crisscrosses, and makes all sorts of fancy figures in the grass. I think he's pretty smart!

A veteran letter carrier says that he has walked his rounds every day, except Sundays and off days, for fifty years, and never has he been bored by his labor.

"People always are glad to see me," he relates. "We postmen, you know, are carriers of good news. If that was not so people would not be glad to see us coming. Yes, sir, in the long run the good news always outweighs the bad. There are more births than deaths, more health than sickness, more marriages than divorces. I've handed over millions of letters and more than half the time I've seen happy expressions on the faces of the people receiving them. I've seen my town grow, change its character. I've carried out announcements of a baby's birth, and then twenty years later carried out the wedding invitations for that same baby. The romances I've seen would fill a big book! We letter carriers can tell when one is on the way. There'll be a lot of letters for a certain girl, and after a while she is out on the porch waiting each morning to see what is in the mail for her.

"Even in this depression folks are glad to see me. It must be that even now good news is the rule and not the exception. That doesn't surprise me, for I've walked through several of these depressions. This one isn't the worst one, either. Maybe it is if you are thinking of its effect upon the big fellows, but I'm sure there is less suffering now than there was in some of the others. Why, even in the bread lines these days men are well dressed. I did not see a man all last winter who was cold for the want of clothes. Years ago, though, I used to see a lot of poor fellows shivering because they had no overcoats and not much of anything on their backs.

"It's something, isn't it, to be the first to deliver a lot of good news to hundreds of people every day? I think it is! And I think it's right interesting to watch streets change, to watch people grow up, to be a daily caller at hundreds of homes and offices."

A man with such a view-point is not likely to go stale. His work is his hobby.

Some time ago I was asked to address the sales force of a great department store. The man who invited me said a lot of his people were gloomy, and he wished I would figure out some way to arouse them. I studied the situation and it seemed clear to me that this sales force needed a fine hobby to ride.

"Some of you have become discouraged," I said to them, "because results are not what you would like them to be. Therefore you have let down in your efforts. Maybe you have depended too much upon results to keep you in the proper state of mind. Well, hard times came along, and in hard times we often have to get our fun out of effort. It is a pleasure merely to do one's best, even if nothing happens. I suggest, therefore, that each of you become genuinely interested in effort. Make it your hobby to put forth the very best effort you are capable of. Set your 'effort goal' very high, and you will find it a grand and glorious feeling every time you live up to your own standard of perfect effort. I have a strong idea that by reversing things, that is, by seeking happiness in effort instead of in result, you soon may find results surprisingly good. The very thing you have been missing may be attained by striving for something else. Put the emphasis on the *means*, then see what the *end* will be.

"On my way here to speak with you I imagined myself as employed in this store, and I put down a list of things I'd do. Here are my ideas:

"1. I'd arrive at work on time, or ahead of time, keen and alert from a good night's rest.

"2. I'd leave my home problems, my financial problems and my social problems outside the store. I recall a locomotive engineer who had a very hard run, but always at home he was placid. Some one asked him why he never seemed nervous, and his reply is worth thinking about. 'I always leave my engine in the round house,' said he. 'I found years ago that I didn't need it here at home.'

"3. I'd put in an honest effort every minute in the interest of my employer. This would be good for him, and better for me.

"4. I'd make it my duty to see that every person who came to me in store hours was treated with the same courteous consideration I'd show to a guest in my home.

"5. I'd show myself superior in self-control, in manners, to those disagreeable customers who so often torment a sales force.

"6. I'd avoid idle gossip and criticism of others.

"7. I'd study and make notes of the wishes of my customers, and report these to my superiors.

"8. I'd do unto customers as I would that they should do unto me if our situations were reversed.

"9. I'd spend a part of my spare time in studying to make a better merchant of myself.

"10. No gum-chewing for me in work hours.

"11. And no slangy talk with customers.

"12. I'd never go into a huddle with my fellow employees to talk over personal matters while customers were awaiting attention.

"13. I'd be especially careful not to hurt the feelings of those customers who have very little money.

"14. I'd treat every customer as though he were the best customer the store ever would have.

"Those fourteen points," I continued, "would be my guide if I were employed in this or any other store. Jobs are scarce, and my effort would be to make mine necessary to the store. Employees who are producing profits are the last to be let out. Employees who show the spirit necessary to a revival of trade, will be the first to win promotion when the better days arrive."

I told them, then, of some experiences and observations of mine. I have a friend who travels and who buys nearly all of his clothes in a small city away from his home. I asked him why he did this.

"Years ago," said he, "when I was a kid

just starting out I made that town selling hardware. I lost my personal baggage en route there one day, and found myself with nothing except the suit I had on. My house was a little one, and I so new that I dreaded to wire back for money. I told the leading merchant of my trouble, and he looked me over, then said he'd take a chance on me. He outfitted me on credit, invited me to go to his home with him for dinner and wished me luck when I left. I figure that I've spent well over a thousand dollars in his store since that experience. Maybe two thousand. And I've told about his store hundreds of times. Deliberately I made it my business to see that this merchant was rewarded."

Decent treatment works like that. It brings its rewards. And careless treatment brings its penalties. Another friend of mine went into a shoe store one day with his small brother. His father, a minister, had just moved to the town, and the older boy explained to a clerk that his little brother needed a pair of shoes, but he'd have to ask that they take a check given him by his father. He even gave references. The price of the shoes was three dollars, the check was for four.

"You don't think I'd take a check from a strange boy, do you?" asked the clerk.

"But you could call up Doctor So and So," said the boy. "He knows my father."

"I'm afraid there's nothing doing," said the clerk.

The youngster's feelings were badly hurt. He went out of that store in humiliation, and he never went back. His family, consisting of five fine brothers and sisters, both parents and an aunt, shared his hurt with him, and though they lived for twelve years in the town, not one of them ever bought a pair of shoes in that store. A thoughtless clerk, lacking in imagination as well as in manners, cost his employer many hundreds of dollars the day he turned that boy away.

You never can tell the potentialities of the customer. The only safe course is to treat every one courteously, wisely and even flatteringly.

When considering hobbies for people who work, I like to think of a story I heard years ago. Three men, so the story runs, were cutting stone for St. Paul's Cathedral in London. A stranger came along and asked what they were doing.

"Cutting stone," said the first.

"Trying to make a few shillings," answered the second.

"*I'm* helping Sir Christopher Wren build a cathedral," declared the third.

That's the winning idea! No matter what I may be doing I can think of it as important. For it is important—to me.

Chapter VIII

A SOCIETY FOR THE SHALLOW-MINDED

After one of my talks last year in California a man asked what my profession was.

"I make my living, that is, my money income," I answered, "by selling life insurance. I make my happiness by trying to be worth something to others and to myself. And I've been introduced as a Trouble Bouncer."

"A what?"

"A Trouble Bouncer. You know, one of the fellows who bounces undesirable persons out of restaurants and hotels. The man who introduced me said my profession was to bounce trouble out of life."

"How?"

"By the simple expedient of not letting it in."

I saw he was not satisfied. There was something on his mind, so we withdrew from the others present and talked a while. The man was manager of a chain grocery store, and was ashamed of his job. His wife, also, was ashamed of it.

"Did you ever sling groceries over a counter?" he asked.

"I certainly have," I answered.

"Well, then, you know that a man doesn't have to be very deep to do that?"

"What do you mean, very deep?"

"I mean he doesn't have to use his head much. My wife says we should get into something intellectual. She is always telling me about other fellows who tried to marry her. One of them is a bank officer now, another a lawyer, and then there's the one who writes stuff."

"Do you want me to be honest in what I say to you? To be absolutely frank?"

"Sure."

"What you need is not an intellectual job, as you call it, but an intellectual attitude toward the one you now have. You are engaged in an essential work. We'd starve if food was not distributed to us in the cities. You are in a growing industry. There is every chance for promotion. There is every reason for pride in your progress so far, and for hope of greater progress. You're lucky and don't know it! And tell your wife, when you go home, that one of the ablest executives in America has said—a lot of them have said—that they look for wife-made men. They know that a wife can make or break a husband. I think you and your wife need to start over again in your attitude toward life and toward your job. You chain-store men have survived the depression far better than most others. Suppose you didn't have any job at all?

"Yes," I continued. "If I were in your situation, I'd either start all over again in my view-point, or I'd resign and turn my job over to some one who wants it and who is worthy to hold it. If it is an evidence of deep-mindedness to be ashamed of honest work, I suggest that you become shallow-minded in your attitude. Make your mind so shallow that there isn't room in it for false pride, for envy of others, for sourness."

I've met many men like this one, some in my own line. I've heard such talk as this:

"What are you doing these days?"

"Well, just at the moment I'm selling insurance, but I have other plans for the spring."

Why wait until spring if you have other plans? The time to do the right thing is now. The time to give an honest day's work is to-day, and no man can give an honest day's work if his mind is all cluttered up with inharmonious thoughts, with silly pride, with regrets that he did not start off in something else. It is every man's duty to be honest, and it is his duty to be happy. He can be neither if he is working at his job with only part of his capacity, while the rest of it is being used up in worrying, in shame or in envy.

Without qualification I am proud of my work, and I am proud of the very simple, common-sense view-point that has enabled me to succeed in it. In my book, *A Fortune to Share,* I told of this view-point and how it made me over. In my talks I have passed out this fortune for any who might wish it. Numerous requests have come to me these past few years for statements of my philosophy, and unnumbered hundreds of persons have told me they were helped by it. I can not but conclude, therefore, that the simple elemental discovery I made is good for many persons. I discovered that I was going through life studying about something—about the ideal attitude toward life. Then I reasoned that if I could go a step further and *be,* that is, reflect in all my thoughts and acts, that ideal attitude I might find a very high order of happiness. Instead of thinking about courage, I would be courage—live it. Instead of yearning for patience, I became patient. Instead of dreaming of what a fine thing tolerance is, I became tolerant. All those things which seemed to me fine, I tried to reflect in my mind, my heart and in my conduct. It was this attitude, and not native ability that has brought me the many blessings for which I am so profoundly grateful. Instead of going about my affairs as a discontented human, I go about them as the exemplification, so far as within my power lies, of the qualities which I admire most, those affirmative, beautiful qualities upon which all progress is based. There was a time when I used up my energy wishing for things, but now I use my energy in claiming and being the things I had previously only wished for.

Some persons do not understand this attitude, and doubtless some do not believe it. Soon after *A Fortune to Share* appeared a very able reviewer gave it generous space and then said, in conclusion, that I was a "shallow-minded bore." Did that hurt me? Not in the least. It was merely another opportunity for me to prove to myself that what happens outside me is of no importance unless I permit it to affect my inner self. This critic was doing his duty, "calling 'em as he saw 'em," just as I had done mine. I was grateful to him for his attention, so I wrote him this letter:

"Dear Editor:

"After generous reference to my book, *A Fortune to Share*, your review contains in part this statement: 'He has no conception that he himself is a shallow-minded bore.' I hope you will not think me facetious when I openly acknowledge that I have a very distinct conception of myself as being a 'shallow-minded bore.'

"Several years ago I was broad-minded and I might say, deep-minded. As a matter of fact, my mind was so broad and deep that it was easy for most of the woes of human existence to find lodgment therein. Self-pity, sickening fear, bewilderment, stewing and worrying about business, regretting the past and doubting the future, discontent and unhappiness were all there in abundance.

"Then came a day when something within me rebelled against all this 'junk' and I suddenly found my mind filled with an intelligent resistance to these things. Understanding, courage, unselfishness and the determination to succeed took occupancy of my mind so completely that all grief and disaster were crowded out.

"Of course, a transition of this kind is very boresome to those who love misery. The country generally is getting ready to settle down and enjoy a good hard winter and does not want to be disturbed by optimism and good cheer. Business as yet has not suffered sufficiently to resist the tendency toward depression with a powerful concerted attack of right thinking and right acting and so we are still in turmoil and confusion.

"I have become so 'shallow-minded' that in the midst of stock-market crashes, bank failures and the cry of poor business, I find myself unafraid and undismayed. The negative and fearful thinking that is paralyzing business and filling individuals with despair simply can not find room in my shallow mind. And the rather interesting part of it is that business with me is very good.

"I am honestly grateful to you for reviewing my book and hope that you will not consider this a disgruntled reply. I am sincere in all that I say.

"Sincerely yours,
(Signed) "VASH YOUNG"

The incident gave me an idea. I took it up with some of my friends, and they agreed it was entertaining. Therefore I said I would form a Society for the Shallow-Minded. There are NO DUES, NO FEES, NO OBLIGATIONS, other than to LIVE IN REBELLION AGAINST DEPRESSION, POOR BUSINESS AND UNHAPPINESS. The only requirement is that your mind shall become so shallow that fear, worry, discontent, discouragement can not find lodgment in it. The benefits are PEACE AND HARMONY AT HOME, SUCCESS IN BUSINESS, GOOD HEALTH AND A COURAGEOUS OUTLOOK ON LIFE.

The creed of the Society is set forth in these fifteen points:

1. I will get up in the morning thanking God for what I have instead of asking Him to give me more.

2. I will try to make somebody happy for the day before leaving the house.

3. I will disregard the weather. I can't do anything about it anyway.

4. I will go out to "give," and not to "get."

5. I will not indulge in or encourage pessimistic talk.

6. I will strive to forget self and think of the other fellow.

7. (If an employer) I will endeavor to

demonstrate to my employees that we are in business to stay.

8. I will assure faithful employees that their jobs are safe.

9. I will encourage and appreciate better service on the part of careless employees.

10. (If an employee) I will demonstrate to my employer and the public that I appreciate my job.

11. I will prove by my work that I am being paid for RIGHT THINKING.

12. I will be willing to demonstrate to my employer my thinking by my acting at any time during the day.

13. I will be a booster instead of a knocker and kicker.

14. I will strive to prove by my works that I am in the best business in the world.

15. Finally, I WILL ENLIST ALL MY THINKING IN FAVOR OF PROGRESS!

Want to join?

Chapter IX

THE FUTURE

Everywhere people are wondering about the future. Business organizations are uncertain in their policies. Individuals glance fearfully ahead.

"What does the future have in store for us?" they ask. That question, to millions of men and women, has become the most important of the day; but to my way of thinking it is the wrong one to ask. The mere asking of it comes perilously close to an admission of defeat. Certainly it is an admission of doubt, and doubt always weakens action. The question we should be asking ourselves to-day is not the passive, almost negative, "What does the future have in store for us?"

but the aggressive, positive query, "What do we have in store for the future?"

This is no time for wringing our hands impatiently, furrowing our brows with the frowns of resentment and regret, clouding our vision with gloom and pessimism while waiting for the future to pour riches into our laps. Riches, whether material or spiritual, never follow such an attitude of mind and heart. But in this chapter I am not thinking much about material wealth. Perhaps already I have given it too much space, considering its relative unimportance. Material possessions have been taken away from a great many fine people, and I am not discounting the fact that this has caused mental anguish, and perhaps some physical hardships. Often a man is not at fault when he loses his money. Many an able man goes through with this earthly experience without ever having acquired much monetary wealth, and for this no one can censure him. But if a man loses spiritual wealth, or if he goes through with his earthly adventure without having acquired it, he is—well, he is indeed unfortunate.

The greatest riches—by far the greatest riches—are those of the mind and of the heart, and these riches in inexhaustible degree are offered to every one of us. Every person has it within his power to become great in heart, in character. Perhaps the world never will be made aware of this greatness, but what of that? The first ambition of every one should be to lift his own thinking to the highest attainable plane. In the realm of the spirit, in the values of the heart, the poorest peasant may achieve nobility equal to that of the noblest nobleman. This is the priceless opportunity given to each of us by our Creator. This is the wealth which is without limit, and which is free. This is a Golden Standard which can not be affected by any business collapse, and which brings peace and happiness beyond understanding.

Therefore I say the question for each of us to ask himself is, "What do *I* have in store for the future?"

Some of the gloomier of the gloomy prophets have predicted that a final grand financial crash would descend upon us. My reply to them is, "What of it?" I do not believe it, but if the smash comes it can carry away nothing but material things. Life will go on. Spiritual values will remain unharmed. Other structures will arise to take the place of those discarded, and they will be better structures. We must go forward. Progress is the law. Nothing can destroy its foundation stones—love, courage, energy. Sometimes we may forget these great virtues, sometimes we may permit false elements to enter into our minds and hearts and replace, for a bit, those eternal verities, but the verities themselves always survive, and sooner or later we seize upon them again and resume our upward march. I wonder if we have not fallen into the wretched habit of accepting false valuations? And I wonder if we are not now prepared to mend this error?

"I think the depression is about over," a friend said to me.

"What makes you think that?" I asked.

"Because I am so tired of it?" he answered, "And every one else is, too."

If you study it long enough you will find something profound in that statement. This friend—and how many others?—is tired of his own unhappiness and worry, hence is ready to revolt against them, ready to strike out anew in the reconquest of lasting, spiritual values.

"I like the depression," another man said.

"Why?"

"Because it has given me a sense of hardihood. I feel as if I am fighting for something now."

And that statement, too, is worthy of study. There is a turning, unquestionably there is a turning to courage, to higher virtues all along the line. A lot of interesting things will happen these next few years, and my guess is that most of them will be good. Let the financial debacle be ever so bad, it nevertheless will sink into unimportance if it serves to bring on a spiritual renaissance. There never will be wholesale starvation in America. There never will be a time when we freeze in the snows of winter. These things are just not going to happen! We have had a great deal more than we actually needed. Even now we have a very good supply of the necessities of life. It is time for us to begin thinking of what we have, of what we may have, and stop grieving for what we have lost. Let's spring out of this mental mess we are in!

I like to believe that no matter how great the business chaos, I still have it within my power to be richer than any monarch on his throne, unless that monarch happens to have the same ideas as those by which I try to live. The finest traits of character the world has known are available to me—and to you—right now.

I read of Washington. Such recognition as the world gave and always will give to him can not be mine, nor one-millionth part of it. But I can have his honesty and courage, and I will be secretly satisfied with them, even though history never will mention my name. I read of Lincoln, and again I am made to realize the enormous gulf between his worth to the world and mine, yet I can achieve the compassion that was Lincoln's, and can be happy with this without the recognition which was his. I read of Lee and know that never can I be a hero even to those who fought in a losing cause. But Lee was a man of poise. I can have that, and rejoice privately in it. I read of Theodore Roosevelt and smile at my own feeble efforts as compared with his stirring accomplishments, and yet at the same time I realize that I can make use of energy to the fullest possible degree, just as he made use of it. The difference in recognition accorded makes no difference to me because I am happy in the possession of fine qualities, without any worldly acclaim attached to them.

When I was in school the teachers used to tell us that the presidency of the United States was within reach of every boy in the room. In theory that no doubt was true, but I think the emphasis of those teachers was wrongly placed. Also I think that many people to-day who read biography fail to read it aright. Some read with a view to winning, if possible, some of the recognition accorded to the great; others read merely for entertainment. I read with a view to discovering which fine traits of character possessed by the great are within my reach. I try to be, in my own privacy, like those whom I most admire. Ability to win acclaim is given to very few, but ability to be equal to the noblest in character is given to every one. This is our guarantee that success, that happiness is within the reach of every one. I know it is platitudinous to say that virtue is its own reward, but I have no objection to platitudes. They usually are true; if they were not, they would not have become platitudes. Indeed, I am very credulous about all the good things said of life. My friends say I am the most credulous man in the world, and I take that as a compliment. When I read in my Bible what Jesus said to Nicodemus—"Verily, verily, I say unto thee, Except a man be born again, he cannot see the kingdom of God"—I believe this applies to me, also; and the statement, "The Kingdom of God is within you," I take to mean that *my* kingdom of God is within *me*.

All of this seems to be saying to us now, as it has been saying these centuries and will continue to say, that we must be starting over again continually, striving for ever toward finer appreciation of values and toward higher goals. Every day I think of these things, and wonder what I can do about them. Then I recall that stirring challenge, that magnificent promise in the eighth verse of the fourth chapter of James:

"Draw nigh to God, and he will draw nigh to you."

THE END